I Know You're Hurting

Lauren Stratford

HARVEST HOUSE PUBLISHERS
Eugene, Oregon 97402

I KNOW YOU'RE HURTING

Copyright © 1989 by Lauren Stratford
Published by Harvest House Publishers
Eugene, Oregon 97402

Library of Congress Cataloging-in-Publication Data

Stratford, Lauren
    I know you're hurting / Lauren Stratford.
    ISBN 0-89081-773-1
    1. Consolation.   2. Suffering—Religious aspects—Christianity.
  I. Title.
  BV4905.2.S76   1989
  248.8'.6—dc20   89-35233
                                               CIP

Printed in the United States of America.

To Jesus
who is healing my hurts.

And to the countless others
who are still hurting.

Lord, let us recover
and be filled with happiness.

My forever thanks:

...to Brother and Sister, who continue to stand by my side. As always, I love you!

...to my newly-found birth relatives, for your acceptance of me.

...to the many at Westbrook Chapel and Tetelestai Christian Center who faithfully uphold me in prayer.

...to Elaine Alexander, my therapist, for hanging in there with me through the storm.

...to the doctors and nurses who worked so unselfishly to save my life. A special thanks to Karen Collier, the nurse who often sat by my bedside reading the promises of God to me.

...to Rachel Gaman and Barbara Long, my hospital social workers, who have held my hand more times than I can remember.

...to Lela Gilbert. I prayed for an editor who would understand the needs of the hurting. The Lord graciously answered with you.

...to the gang at Harvest House, for always being there for me.

...to Stormie Omartian and Janet Hinde, for your loving contributions to my manuscript.

...to Dr. Catherine Gould and Dr. Lyn Laboriel, for your compassionate commitment to the hurting.

...to the precious ones who allowed me to share their private pains and hurts with my readers.

...to three little ones: Joey, Carly and Lindy. I hold you in my heart.

I am blessed!

FOREWORD

✦

I have received thousands of letters from people telling me about the most horrible abuses in their lives, but none worse than those revealed in a letter from Lauren Stratford a few years ago. She was not writing as someone without hope, for she had already found that and was well on the road to restoration. What she sought was my advice as to the extent she could share the truth of her past in an autobiography she was contracted to write for Harvest House. Because of my own experience in writing a book on child abuse, she wanted to know how much I thought people could bear to hear without becoming so sickened they would put the book down and stop reading. I encouraged her to tell everything in order for her readers to know the depths from which she had been rescued and how far the Lord had brought her. She did just that, handling the worst incidents with care, and the result was her greatly successful book *Satan's Underground.*

Lauren found, as I have too, that after introducing someone to the idea there is hope for their lives, they need to know what steps to take next. This book answers that need. I know from experience that writing such a book is a painful endeavor and there is no glamour, fame, fortune or fun in it enough to be a draw for that kind of punishment. It is purely a labor of love—love for people whose souls are aching.

I Know You're Hurting is a book of comfort and encouragement to any person experiencing emotional pain, from an author who understands the depths of suffering and discouragement. But it is not a Band-Aid to protect wounds from more hurt, as important as that is in the beginning of a fresh injury. Rather it encourages exposure of the wound to the flushing, cleansing and restoring process. She doesn't let us deny the pain, but rather shows us how to face it.

The fact that Lauren is alive, has a sound mind and has written this book is evidence that God is real, that Jesus is the Deliverer and Restorer and there is no hurt beyond His healing. Because of what she has lived through, she causes us to think about the unthinkable, to believe the unbelievable, and to speak about the unspeakable atrocities of our time. The things that happened to Lauren are real and they are happening to people right now. Because of her we cannot ignore it in others or deny it in ourselves.

Over the past few years, she has moved from victim to survivor to overcomer and in the process has become God's instrument in setting free those bound and imprisoned by the paralyzing devastation of their past. Lauren Stratford was born for such a time as this.

—Stormie Omartian

CONTENTS

◆

Foreword

A Special Word to the Reader

1. Satan's Underground:
   Tragedy to Triumph 11

2. Broken Pottery 23

3. It's Just You and Me, God! 45

4. I Wait with You 59

5. Intimacy with God 69

6. "But Lord, I'm So Weak!" 87

7. Oh, the Masks We Wear! 99

8. The Garden of My Tears 121

9. Touch Me, Heal Me 135

10. God, Don't Ask Me to Be a Job! 149

11. When Trouble Comes, Where Are You? 167

12. God Wastes Nothing—Even This! 183

13. I Give You My Comfort 197

14. Born from Affliction 213

15. Working Through It 227

16. Epilogue: New Healings 247

A SPECIAL WORD
TO THE READER

When the questions you ask have no answers.
When everything has fallen apart.
When nothing makes sense anymore.
When your heart is breaking.
To whom do you turn?
Or do you keep silent, gritting your teeth,
    until your pain becomes unbearable?

I wish I had all the answers. How I wish I did! How much easier it would be to write this book! I heard someone talking about hurts and healing on the radio a few months ago. "Do you want to get rid of your hurt?" he asked. "Then just do it!"

I thought to myself, *If only it were that simple. It surely hasn't been a "just do it" formula for me.* It would be wonderful to be able to provide three easy steps to healing, but I can't. However, I do know that there is healing for our hurts!

I don't say that lightly. If you've read my first book, *Satan's Underground*, you know that I speak from my own experience. Jesus can heal even the worst of hurts. Yes, even yours! And since I'm still on my own pilgrimage to healing, I'm eager to share what I'm learning with you. Whether the process seems difficult or slow, comforting or exciting, one thing is certain. Jesus walks with us, His hand in ours, and we are all moving ahead together.

I know you're hurting. Many of you can echo the pain of a woman who wrote these words in a letter:

"I am a Christian, but I'm more depressed now than ever. I have never been able to talk to anyone as I should have. I am losing my faith, because I feel that God does not hear me, or is just forsaking me."

This dear woman ended her letter with a cry from the bottom of her heart. Her last sentence was, "Could you help me?"

So hurting . . . and so alone! Yet she's reaching out for help.

I wonder every time I receive another letter of pain and hurt, "Can my words—can anyone's words—heal their pain?" The answer is all-too-clear. Only Jesus can do the healing. I can but point the way to Him. I called this woman a few days ago and told her that it was for her and the many who are like her that I was writing this book.

When I began to feel that the Lord wanted me to write about the healing of emotional pain, my first reaction was, "Lord, how can I write a book to the hurting when I'm still hurting? What can I say that will help others in the midst of their pain and suffering?"

The Lord waited patiently until I was finished. But then, as only He can do, He began to speak to my heart in a still and gentle voice. He let me see that I could not say to others "God will be with you in your pain," unless I was willing to be in the same place with them. To make matters worse, I began to feel that I was going to have to live through many of the things I would be writing about. I really didn't want that! I voiced my protest loudly!

"Lord, haven't I been through enough? Isn't my survival through a life of abuse and horror proof enough that You do care for Your own?"

"Yes, my child." There was that still voice again. "You have been through enough. But your story has been one of such miracles that many people think you're not hurting any longer. They believe you've been instantly healed of all emotional and physical pain."

Sounds pretty good to me! I thought. But in my heart I knew that I was still going through a lot of healing. I knew that the Lord was right. My words would have more of an impact if I could say, "Yes, I am still hurting. I am still healing. And for that very reason I am able to share in your hurts."

None of us is immune to the afflictions of this life. None of us has reached a plateau where we are untouchable by the evils around us. And that includes me!

Even everyday life can be a struggle, and simple daily problems can add up to insurmountable mountains. It isn't just the horrific troubles that spell disaster. It doesn't take the tragedy of murder or a terminal illness to plant seeds of doubt—seeds like, "Does God care about me?" and "If He really loves me, why is this happening?"

I heard someone once say, "Welcome to the real world, folks!" The fact is, we do inhabit a very real and troubled planet. Our adversary, the devil, does roam the earth, seeking out whom he may destroy. We are subject to all kinds of tribulation.

You and I will know what it is to hurt as long as we're alive. But I stand here to tell you that there is one who sees and feels our hurt and is waiting to heal. His Name is Jesus Christ, "Jehovah Rophe," your Healer.

My prayer is that as you read these pages, you will be ministered to at the point of your pain, grief and disillusionment. My heart's desire is that you will come to know Jesus as the Healer of your broken heart.

– 1 –

Satan's Underground: Tragedy to Triumph

✦

Dear Editor,

I read the book, *Satan's Underground*. Lauren told a lot about Satan's church's methods. These things cannot be made public. Satan's members don't let anyone break free. *No one!* If you can, would you please write me back and let me know, is Lauren really free? Is Lauren still alive? I just don't believe anyone is ever free from Satan's people!

This letter, from a woman named Heather, was one of the first responses I received after my autobiography, *Satan's Underground*, was released in March of 1988. No words of my own could reveal the heart of a wounded soul more than the letter from this dear woman. No response has made me more thankful that I took, what was at the time, a calculated risk to my personal safety. And no response has made me more thankful that I worked so hard in overcoming the gnawing fear of what the public would think of me after reading about my experiences.

Throughout my life, my abusers taught me to "Shut up, keep quiet and never tell anyone." For years, I did just that. And when I finally did risk "telling it all" (or as much as I thought necessary), I doubted that I would

11

hear from more than a few victims of similar abuses and atrocities.

Little did I know that hundreds of victims were desperately waiting for someone to crack the door open, revealing the secrets of the heinous underground. Yes, I surely knew they were out there. But I couldn't have guessed how many men and women would take the risk of speaking out themselves.

How well I remember praying with my editors at Harvest House, holding hands across the conference table during the final editing of *Satan's Underground*. We asked God to make the book all that He wanted it to be, and prayed that it would deeply minister to victims of hurt and abuse. We wiped tears from our eyes, feeling the burden of children and adults who remained imprisoned within their abusive situations.

When the letters began to come in, not just in ones and twos but by the dozens, I could only lift up my head and say, "Thank You, Lord. Thank You." And when the Lord gave me the privilege of responding to those letters and writing, "Yes, I am free! You can be, too!" the book that I was so fearful of anyone reading became a blessing. I was assured that it was being used to bring hope to victims who were in bondage and without hope.

Hope was given to victims like Heather, who felt she was one step beyond rescue. Her healing can be no more vividly chronicled than through portions of three ensuing letters.

> I'm so happy to hear you're alive and well. I can now say I know someone who got out! But I still feel like I belong to Satan. Now I see from your story that it *can* be done. I want to be free someday too!

After I responded again, she confided to me about her personal involvement in satanism and about her fears of trying to escape the cultists' influence. She ended her letter with:

> The group I was involved in always told me if I ever left, everything I try will fall back on me. So I have no right to ask Jesus to be my Lord and Master. Like they said, Satan will always be with me waiting for the right time to take what is his—*Me!*

Praise God, He is the victor even in impossible situations. After much prayer and more correspondence with Heather, one of her most recent letters was the testimony of another precious soul whose life was snatched out of Satan's hands. A new and transformed Heather wrote:

> I have been reading your book over and over. For the first time in my life, I feel like Jesus is hearing me. I feel like something is pulling Satan away from me. I have strength now. Jesus is with me!

What a remarkable change! God reached out to Heather where she was—one step beyond—and is now restoring her to wholeness. The cost of living through the hell of Satan's underground and the writing and reliving of those memories was paid in full when I received Heather's last letter! If no other victories had been reported, I still would not trade one horror for the joy of knowing another victim of Satan's underground had been rescued.

I'm writing this book to persons who are hurting badly. Because I'm still healing from my own past hurts, I occasionally refer to incidents I described in *Satan's Underground.* Some of you, I'm sure, have not read the story of my life. For this reason, I need to go back and share the highlights with you.

Satan's Underground is a difficult book to read. I wrote the book in tears, and many have read it in tears. It was not purposely meant to stir such emotions. In fact, many potentially sensational situations were left out, because our purpose was not to produce a provocative book that dramatically delved into the hidden evils of this world. *Satan's Underground* portrays certain ugly incidents for two reasons only. First, to say, "Yes, these things do happen and there are children and adult victims of these crimes." But even more importantly the book proclaims, "There is a sure escape from this evilness through the Lord Jesus Christ."

Child victims of physical and sexual abuse are hurting, and hurting desperately. It is safe to assume that at least twenty percent of you, and probably more, have been sexually abused as children. Chances are, you've never told anyone, and you're suffering now because you've never dealt with that abuse.

I was one of those children.

Child pornography is estimated to be a two-to-three-billion-dollar-a-year industry in this country. Unfortunately, some of you are victims of this hideous, insidious evil.

I was one of those children.

Although ritualistic abuse seems to be one of the new crimes of the '80's, it has been around since Bible times when children were sacrificed to the god, Molech. Today, two to six-year-olds are telling stories of ritualistic abuse at preschools, daycare centers and at their satanist father's hands. Adult victims are reliving similar memories. Some even recall the sacrifice of their own babies.

I am one of those adults.

The Tragedy

I was born to a man and woman who were in love, but

unmarried. I've been told that my father wanted to keep me, but that my mother wanted no children—ever! She agreed to marry my father only if I was given up. My father reluctantly agreed, and I became the infant baby girl of another set of parents.

The adoption spelled disaster from the beginning. Within a few years, my father left the home because he was being abused regularly by my mother. He never fought back or defended himself, and he knew only to run. That was fine for him, but I was left to receive the brunt of my mother's wild outbursts of rage.

When I was six years of age, she allowed me to be used to gratify the sexual pleasures of men who hung around our house doing odd jobs and menial work. Small as I was, I was stricken with shame and guilt, and a horrible feeling of being very dirty—too dirty ever to feel clean again. I was like a piece of shattered pottery, lying on the floor in a thousand tiny pieces. The control of my body, my mind, and my spirit had already begun.

The ravaging that went on behind closed doors was well orchestrated, and quickly expanded into child pornography. I entered my teenage years a programmed robot, functioning and performing on command.

Since the release of *Satan's Underground*, I've learned that one of the most difficult parts of my story for the readers to understand was my inability to find help. It has been very troubling to me, for I explained it in the book as well as I could. It is a situation where words are simply inadequate. I voiced my frustration to the Lord Jesus often, asking Him to give me the right words to say, not as an excuse, but words that would describe the reality as it was.

One day in Detroit, I was doing an interview with Foster Braun on WCM radio. He and I were talking about the conditioning that takes place in children who have been subjected to long-standing sexual abuse and child pornography. Out of the clear blue, Foster summed up what I had been trying to say for a whole year while writing *Satan's Underground.*

"Lauren, they didn't hold a gun to your head. They didn't tie you to the bed posts. And yet you were a captive. It sounds like there came a time when your abusers no longer needed to put visible walls up. There were *internal* fences that kept you locked in."

Those two words, "internal fences," instantly broke through the communications barrier! When Foster spoke those words, I was so eager to go with that concept that I interrupted him.

"They could have let me go. By that time, when I was eighteen or nineteen, they could have said, 'You're free. Go live your own life.' I would have lived on the street and never said a word to anybody. I was so afraid of these people. I believed everything they told me, and I acted accordingly. I didn't rebel. I didn't try to get help after that. I was really like a trained robot plugged into their computer."

Then Foster added two more words that further clarified my inability to "run for the woods." He said, "Lauren, it sounds to me like you were captive to not only internal fences, but invisible walls. You were kept a prisoner of a lie . . . and very effectively!"

Foster will never know how encouraged I was by his understanding. I knew I would never forget his words, but I couldn't wait to get back to my hotel to write them down anyway. They were priceless gems of truth for which I had been desperately searching.

When I was in my late teenage years and in my early twenties, I went to college during the week, and was taken to the pornographers on weekends. I had long since learned to live in two totally opposite worlds, acting "appropriately" in each one. Nevertheless, it was horribly strenuous to pretend that the ugly world of pornography, with all its depravity and abuse, wasn't really happening.

Victor, the head pornographer, regarded me in a crazy sort of way as his woman. It wasn't long before he became bored with his other illegal businesses, and entered into the world of satanism. Where Victor went, I went! Voluntarily or involuntarily, it mattered not to him. He simply made sure that I accompanied him as he descended into the pit of hell.

I have heard one of the more recognizable and well-known satanists in this country say that their rituals are "beautiful and wonderful and ones of which to be proud." Perhaps to a satanist, that would seem so. But let me make something very clear. I never saw anything that even resembled beauty, and there was surely nothing there of which I could ever be proud! I saw evil. I saw disgusting, degrading atrocities committed in the name of Satan. I felt the very presence of the devil himself in everything that was done.

And yet, sadly, the allure of satanism is growing continuously in our society. There are probably at least twenty letters in my files from parents whose teenage sons have joined satanic covens in their high schools. They write that their teenagers' behavior has changed so radically that they are actually frightened, for their own safety as well as that of their children. I've even heard from parents of Christian teenagers who are being enticed, or harassed and threatened, into attending rituals.

Hurting parents. Hurting grandparents. Frustrated therapists. Concerned pastors. All of these are being touched by satanism, and all are becoming victims in one way or another. The children and adults who have been abused by people who call themselves satanists are in critical need of the healing touch of Jesus Christ. Jesus is the only One who can bring complete freedom from the supernatural powers of evil and darkness.

I was one who stood in critical need of intervention. I required help from someone who wasn't afraid to tackle

Satan with the Word of God and intercessory prayer. But that intervention did not come until I had walked through the haunting shadows of satanic rituals with Victor.

I will not dwell on those practices. The purpose of this book is not for the revealing of these kinds of activities. But I will mention a "Joey" in a couple of places. For Joey is one of the deepest hurts in my life.

With that in mind, I must let you know who Joey is. Joey is the son to whom I gave birth after becoming pregnant through sexually abusive practices at a ritual. One day, I may write a book about Joey and the circumstances surrounding other ritual sacrifices, but it is enough for now to tell you that Joey was taken from me at birth and offered to Satan at the age of six months. He was a sacrificial lamb—"a lamb to the slaughter" as my sister, Johanna Michaelsen, has aptly described it.

I also choose to include Joey, because of the scores of other adults who have begun to reveal their own hell of losing a child in the same manner. The loss of any child by any means is a devastating tragedy. We who have lost children need so very badly to be healed of our hurts and restored to wholeness through the Lord Jesus Christ.

Being a victim of the "unthinkable," and the "unbelievable," no matter what that tragedy is, does two things to a person. First of all, we remain victims because our will has been broken. We've seen and felt too much horror. That horror becomes such a dominating force in our lives that the "other world out there" is not even a reality to us. Other ways of living cease to exist.

Secondly, the victim of a continued nightmare sees no way out. It didn't take long for the "no way out, no hope, it's never going to happen" syndrome to become my truth and my reality. How many hurting people have gone through some personal terror and have lost sight of ever getting help; of ever being believed; of ever being thrown a lifeline? How many of us remain, like Foster

Braun said, "captives of internal fences and invisible walls"?

I was controlled through threats and harassments long after I could have escaped, but I was lost in my own fears and my own belief that there was no one who could help me. I couldn't make myself get well—I was too broken! I was just waiting (and even at times, wishing) for someone to sweep up the pieces of my life and dump them in the garbage!

The Triumph!

The Lord had a better idea! I did not belong in a trash bag, the garbage, or the dump. The Lord not only saw me as savable, but He saw me as one whom He could heal and actually use for His glory! He saw in me what I could not see in myself—the finished product.

To effect that end, He led me to Randolph and Johanna Michaelsen, who believed me, accepted me and loved me. They also knew how to wage an all-out war against the strongholds of Satan. It was not easy, but the victory was won! I learned how to stand firm, not only against those who were threatening and harassing me and otherwise controlling me, but against the evil one himself.

I look back at the Lauren Stratford of three and four years ago, and I wonder how she could be the same Lauren Stratford I see today. I echo the words I've sung many times over, "What a wonderful change in my life has been wrought!"

In sharing the miracle of my life with others, numbers of people wrote, "Your story has taught me how to forgive. I hadn't realized how much unforgiveness and bitterness I had toward my father (or whomever they named). Then I read about how you found it necessary to forgive before you could be healed of your past."

Do you know that when I wrote *Satan's Underground*

I never once thought, *I think God is going to use this story to minister to people about the importance of forgiveness?* In fact, I wrote only a few sentences about forgiveness. Yet, God took those words and applied them to the hearts of scores of hurting people who were harboring months and even years of unforgiveness.

Another frequent response also surprised me. "Thank God you wrote about all the problems and trials and hurts that you faced while you were a Christian. Until I read your book, I thought that I was the only Christian who'd had so many bad things happen. I even began to doubt whether I was a Christian, because I've always believed that *no one* suffers that much with Jesus in his life. Now I know I'm normal!"

I never knew so many Christians felt that way. I had always had little else *but* problems, and assumed that all Christians went through a whole lot of suffering. I had learned well the Scripture that says,

Many are the afflictions of the righteous . . .

but it was years before I accepted the last half of the verse:

but the Lord delivereth him out of them all (Psalm 34:19 KJV).

That was the final message in *Satan's Underground*, and it is the beginning message in this book. Never would I have dreamed that God would use the story in *Satan's Underground* to minister to Christians. Every time another Christian comes up to me to thank me for the encouragement and hope they found in the story, I say a quick "thank you" in my heart to Jesus.

The triumph in *Satan's Underground* is not my triumph; it is Jesus Christ triumphing in me. It is Jesus

Christ canceling out defeat and bringing every evil situation into a glorious victory. It is Jesus Christ who is saying, "*I am* the God over *every* situation. And *I am* the God over *your* situation."

For every parent who has written, "My son is about to commit suicide!"

For every adult victim who has written, "There is no way out for me."

For every parent of a ritualistically abused child who has written, "My little girl just told me that we weren't her parents anymore—that Satan is her new father."

For every prisoner who has written, "I molested my little girls and I've lost their love and trust forever."

For every young woman who has written, "My father made me look at his pornography when I was a child, and now I can't get those pictures out of my mind."

> For every person who has poured out
>   the hurts of their heart to me,
> I say to you that there is hope—
>   hope through the healing touch of Jesus
>   Christ!

My dear hurting friend, it is not who I am or what I have done that can make the difference in your life. It is Jesus—who *He* is and what *He* has done—that will bring your healing.

Yes, I did go through hell. I did go through unspeakable hurt. I did make it through Satan's underground. But I did not make it through on my own. I did not find freedom on my own. I am not healing myself. It has only been through Jesus Christ that my miracle has happened. It has only been as I have allowed Him to bear my pain and hurt and hopelessness that healing has begun. I'll say it again, "What I couldn't do, what no one else could do, Jesus is doing!"

How about you? Perhaps your hurts are far different than mine. Perhaps they seem small, yet your tears never seem to stop. Perhaps they seem vast, and huge, and there appears to be no escape. Perhaps you are trapped behind internal fences, unable to see beyond invisible walls.

No matter how broken you are, you are still God's creation, and only He knows how to put you back together again. I believe that through the life I lived, as shared in *Satan's Underground*, I have begun to learn a little bit about God's way of dealing with emotional pain. No matter what the trouble, His answers remain the same. And so it is my prayer that, as I share some of these answers with you, you will find hope and healing for your hurting heart.

– 2 –

Broken Pottery

◆

Broken pottery, Lord.
That's what I am.
  You've broken me,
  Crushed me,
  And I lie in a thousand pieces.
Why the breaking?
Why the crushing?
And why Your silence?
  I cry out to You
  And the darkness becomes darker.
  I listen for Your voice
  Yet I hear nothing.
I am waiting
  waiting
      waiting
My breaking continues.
My hurt deepens.
  When will You mend my brokenness?

You may be nodding your head and saying, "Yes, yes, that's me. I've been there." Or, "I'm there now!"

Let me assure you—you're not alone! There are very few who have escaped the inevitable hurts of living, who bear no scars from emotional battles. Very few have not joined "the walking wounded"—those who struggle from

23

day to day, perhaps from hour to hour—with hearts still bleeding from unhealed hurts. No, you're not alone.

"I've had enough. Take away my life. I've got to die sometime. It might as well be now."

That was the cry of the prophet Elijah. This great man of God had had it! He was so depressed and broken that he lay down beneath a bush and went to sleep, waiting to die.

Perhaps you too have cried out, "God, I've had enough! I can't take any more. If it's not going to get any better, just take my life and let me die now."

In looking back over some of the painful times in my own life, I often think that if I had had the choice of pressing a "live" or "die" button, I would have chosen to "die." Thank God that choosing to die is not quite so simple as pressing a button! In the distress of the moment, any one of us might have been tempted to end it all. This happens, not because we really want to die, but because we want to get away from our hurts.

Sometimes our hurts seem only to deepen and multiply with the passing of time. During those times we know only to cry out, "Lord, get me out of here! Let me die!" Fortunately God, in His infinite wisdom and patience, listens to our desperate cry and whispers lovingly yet firmly, "No, not now, my child. I have promises of hope for you that you have not yet understood. If you will hang on and let me take you through the process of healing, I will reveal these to you."

A few months ago, I reached a point where I was feeling like I just might like to get off the merry-go-round. I asked the Lord if He didn't agree that this was a good time to take me home to be with Him. Life in heaven becomes more and more appealing as life on earth becomes more and more difficult. At that particular moment, heaven really looked like the better alternative!

As usual (I suppose I really didn't expect Him to agree with me!), He said, "Not yet my child. I want you to remain on earth. You have a new book to write. I know part of your healing has been painful and slow, but I'm going to bring other healings into your life that will be a joy to go through."

I didn't fully understand. To be honest, I didn't understand at all! Healing had always been slow and sometimes painful. What this "joy" in healing was, I didn't have a clue!

Our Lord is so gracious. He saw my impatience. He probably even smiled at it, because He knows I'm always impatient to speed up His processes! And, in His kindness and mercy, He gave me a glimpse of what He was talking about.

The Leaning Tower

When I first began my journey back into the "real world," several therapists and counselors, trained in listening and giving sound and practical advice, were very beneficial to me. They listened to me and accepted me the way I was while I was going through the initial traumas of dealing with my hurts. They provided me with a much-needed safety net into which I was able to unload the ugliness I was afraid to entrust to anyone else.

Several years ago, one of my therapists visited Italy. During our first session after she came back home, she handed me a "something." I looked at it inquisitively. It was obviously a replica of what looked like a tower.

"What's this?" I asked.

"I was stopping at the little booths on one of the streets in Pisa, Italy, Lauren, and I saw this replica of The Leaning Tower of Pisa. It reminded me of you so much that I couldn't resist getting it for you."

As I looked it over, I wasn't sure whether that was a

compliment or not! "It looks awfully crumpled, like it's about to fall down."

"That's just the point, Lauren. This tower has gone through earthquakes, severe weather storms and other attacks on it that could have been disastrous. Even though it has cracks and it's tilting to the side because of the damage it has sustained, it refuses to crumble. Scientists say it should have fallen down years ago. They can't explain what keeps it upright. Yet it remains to this day."

I appreciated what she was saying, but I had to ask her, "How does it remind you of me?"

"Lauren, you've gone through so much. You could have crumbled years ago. Yes, you're broken. You're damaged and hurting. Yet you remain!"

I opened my hand and took another look at the tower. "Yes," I thought, "this *is* me. I may be broken. I may be hurt. But I'm still standing!"

I took it home and put it on a shelf. It meant a lot to me. Maybe it meant too much—I don't know. But not long afterward, I couldn't find it. It simply was not where I had put it. Or so I thought.

I moved to another residence a few months ago. What do you think turned up when I started packing? Uh-huh! The replica of The Leaning Tower of Pisa. I unwrapped the tower and put it on the bookshelf in my new study.

No great and mighty miracle happened. The statue didn't zap rays of healing light in my direction as I sat at my desk writing. But every time that feeling of discouragement and heavy weariness began to settle on me, I would turn around and look at it. It reminded me of God's love. Even though I was still feeling quite broken at times, He was keeping me through every stage of my healing. Looking at the little replica, I would give a sigh of relief and think, *Yep, I'm still standing!*

God often uses small messages in big ways to keep a spark of hope alive in our hearts. And so, with His unfailing promise of healing, let's begin to talk about our hurts.

Why Me, Lord?

We state our case. The list is long.

"I can't stand to hurt any longer."
"It never gets any better."
"It's not fair."
"Don't You *hear* me?"
"Don't You *see* me?"
"Where are You?"

And our cries often end with:

"Don't You even love me?"

There we are—sitting underneath a bush like Elijah—feeling alone, abandoned, weary, uncared for, hopeless, unloved, broken.

The vessel of your life has fallen to the ground. It is lying there, smashed to bits. It is so demolished that the tiny fragments are indistinguishable. No matter how you try, you can see no hope of it ever being put together again. Healing seems impossible. You are irreparable!

If that's the way you feel, just remember: *It's okay to be broken.*

I hear the voice of guilt and self-condemnation in so many hurting people. We feel guilty because we aren't whole and well. We feel condemned because we haven't lived up to someone's standard of Christian perfection.

Oh, perhaps it's fine to be a *little* down. Maybe it's all right to feel a *little* depressed—but not for more than a couple of hours. But when we're *really* down, and we can't seem to get ourselves back together again, that's a different story.

Do you know what happens when we feel guilty about our brokenness? We cover it up. We don't let anyone know about it. *Not even God!* We force a smile. We give an "I'm fine" answer. We blink back threatening tears. Our carefully worded prayers dare not speak of our hurts, our pain, our woundedness, our brokenness. We may even find ourselves staying home from church on Sunday, because we fear we might lose our composure in church! I know. I've been there too!

We will talk about the "masks" we wear a little later, but let me assure you of a few important matters right now!

> It's okay to hurt;
> It's okay to feel broken;
> And it's okay to cry out to God
> in anguish.

David did. David the psalmist cried out, "O Lord, from the depths of despair I cry for your help: Hear me! Answer! Help me!" (Psalm 130:1,2 TLB).

We can learn from David. This king of Israel who was close to the heart of the Lord had the assurance that, out of his deepest depths of trouble and affliction, he could give himself permission to cry unto God without guilt or shame! It was David's honesty before God that prevented him from sinking any lower, and that same honesty opened his wounds to the Lord's healing touch.

When he was down, he said he was down. When he felt forsaken, he said he felt forsaken. When he felt like he was going under for the last time, he said so. In fact, it was David who acknowledged to the Lord that he had "become like broken pottery" (Psalm 31:12 NIV). And God rewarded him by attending to his cry.

Are You Broken?

Pottery comes in all different sizes, shapes and colors. Some is beautiful and costly, and some is plain, functional and inexpensive. But whatever its degree of beauty, cost or function, when it becomes broken, it is nothing more than broken pottery—period!

If it was beautiful, its beauty is now lost. If it was costly, it's now worth nothing. If it was of a particular use, it is now of no use. Its brokenness has rendered it useless, ugly and sometimes, no matter the degree of tender loving care that is put back into it, simply beyond repair. That which was valuable is now a piece of junk, not only worthless, but useless.

Do you feel like broken pottery? Has the hurt in your life left you feeling worthless and useless? Do you feel like the nursery-rhyme character, Humpty Dumpty, who all the king's horses and all the king's men couldn't put back together again? Do you feel "unfixable"?

Several years ago, I heard a pastor say, "It's okay to just let go. Perhaps that's the most responsible thing you can do. For underneath you'll find the arms of Jesus waiting to catch you, hold you and sustain you for as long as it takes you to regain your strength. If you don't let go, you'll continue to struggle and fight in your own strength. You'll be trying to do it on your own, and you won't do it very well!" How true those words have been for me.

Beyond Repair

It doesn't matter who or what has broken you—parent, spouse, child, sickness, death, drugs, abuse, failure, finances, sexual sin, loneliness, depression, lost faith, gossip—whatever the circumstances, *broken is broken, and broken needs fixing*.

There can be a sad correlation between clay pottery and the pottery of human life. Not long ago I spoke to an audience of law enforcement, mental health and education professionals. Unknown to me, a number of victims of sexual abuse were also in attendance. After the meeting, several of them came up front to talk with me. Most of them wanted to say, "Thank you for having the courage to share your story," but one young woman stood apart from the rest.

Looking me in the eyes, she started to say something. Before the first word got out, she began to sob, loudly and uncontrollably. The crowd around us grew suddenly quiet. As the woman's sobs filled the room, they seemed to reverberate off every wall, growing louder and more tormented with each passing minute. She finally put her head on my shoulder and clung to me for dear life. For the time being I only knew to put my arms around her and hold her tightly.

Talk about broken pottery! I felt that if I let go of her, her body would fall to the floor and break in a million pieces! So I held on and let her cry her heart out. Most people try to hide their tears and stifle their cries. But this dear woman was so full of hurt and anguish that she was long past the ability to contain her grief.

In a few minutes, I began to hear muffled words between sobs. At first it was difficult to understand her. I finally made out the words, "Broken. I feel so broken. Somebody broke me." The repeated words "broken, broken, broken" began to trail off into more sobbing. I held her as tightly as I could.

It wasn't important for me to know the whys, whos and hows. It was only important that I know she was in desperate need. I spent the next minutes sharing in her brokenness. She finally had let out whatever measure of anguish was necessary to pull herself together enough to loosen her grip on me. I pointed to a couple of chairs and we sat down.

She began to briefly tell me about her life. I learned that she had been severely abused for a prolonged period of time and had only recently begun to deal with the aftereffects in counseling.

Her final sentence before she began to cry again was, "I just can't make myself well. I'm too broken!"

Too broken to stop hurting! Too broken to get well! Without hope. Waiting for the pieces to be swept up and thrown away!

"It's true, dear one," I responded. "You can't heal yourself, but I know someone who can." What a privilege it was to share Jesus with her—Jesus, the Healer of broken hearts. "When you're broken, you can't do anything but hurt. Only the One who created you can put you back together again. The hands of the Master Craftsman will tend to each broken piece, lovingly, gently, carefully, perfectly.

"Jesus knew you before you were born. You were created in His image. He knows the number of hairs on your head. He hears each heartbeat and when your heart begins to break, He shares in your sorrow."

"But I'm just a heap of . . ." She hesitated as if she couldn't find the right word. "A heap of . . . garbage. I feel like a pile of garbage."

"Oh no, honey," I whispered. "God doesn't make garbage." Taking her face in my hands, I looked her squarely in the eyes. "You may feel like you've been broken into tiny pieces and tossed onto the ground, but you'll always be precious in God's sight. No matter how shattered you are, you're still God's creation and He knows how to put you back together again."

And it's true. As the familiar saying goes, "God don't make no junk!" When a beautiful creation of God's handiwork becomes like broken pottery, that creation is still beautiful in God's eyes. The beauty, the value and the usefulness of that person hasn't changed. We need only the touch of the Master's hands on our brokenness to bring restoration.

In a recent sermon, my pastor preached with a vulnerable honesty that encouraged me. At one point he confided, "All week long I've been going to my study early in the morning to pray, and all I've been able to do is fall on my knees and cry 'Help!' for the whole hour."

I thought to myself, "How neat! My pastor is human. He hurts and he's not afraid to admit it, not to God and not to his congregation."

The fact is, there is no one with whom we should feel more comfortable than the Lord. If there is anyone with whom we should feel free to express our deepest anguish without fear of criticism or rejection, it is the Lord. If there is anyone who can identify with heartbreak and torment of heart, it is our wonderful Lord. After all, He was crucified, and He hung on the cross in agony—for you and for me.

In the Garden of Gethsemane, where Jesus went to pray before His betrayal by Judas, Jesus was deeply distressed and troubled. To Peter, James and John, He said, "My soul is overwhelmed with sorrow to the point of death" (Mark 14:34 NIV).

Jesus went a little farther into the garden to pray alone. Feeling the sorrow of His nearing crucifixion, His heart became a bleeding wound, and sweat like drops of blood fell to the ground. Jesus' hurt was further deepened when, bearing the weight of the sins of the world on the cross, He felt the trauma of His own Father turning away from Him. Crying out, "My God, my God, why have You forsaken me?" (Mark 15:34 NIV), He breathed His final breath and died. What sorrow! What torment! What agony and abandonment! Never will there be deeper hurts and suffering than His!

And now He beckons us to turn to Him. He felt His own hurt, and He can fully identify with ours. I point you to Him who, in spite of His hurt and pain, became a triumphant and risen Savior. He offers the same promise of healing and the same resurrection power to you and me.

We need only to whisper the words, "Heal me, Lord, and I shall be healed," and the work is begun. The way He chooses to heal may not be understandable or even felt at the time. The healing may come slowly. The hurt of the brokenness may linger on as the pieces are mending. But whatever time it takes and whatever process of healing we go through, the healing will come!

One Step Beyond

Many broken people have asked me, "What do I do when I'm hurting so badly? I feel like my hurt is one step beyond God's reach."

One step beyond! How many of us have reached that point?

A couple of years ago, I sat in a counselor's office with grief so deep that I was certain it was one step beyond, where no one—not even God could reach it—let alone heal it.

I had been officially told the night before that my birth parents had not been the typical "too young to adequately keep and care for a newborn" stereotypes that I had always imagined. It was that concept that had enabled me to emotionally handle the knowledge that I had been given away as an infant. My parents had done the best thing for me, right?

Wrong! The court records revealed that they were both mature adults who had stable and ongoing employment. It was further disclosed that my birth mother didn't want me, and the only way she would consent to marry my father was if he would agree to give me away.

The last piece of information did me in. I was told that my birth father had committed suicide when I was twelve years of age. That's all I was told at that time, nor could I have handled even one more sentence.

> Hurt beyond healing.
> Angry beyond description.
> Broken beyond repair.
> I was unrescuable!

Sobs began to wrench my body and unending tears began to flow. My confidential intermediary tried to comfort me, but my grief was beyond comforting. I sobbed long into the night hours until I fell asleep in exhaustion.

Awakening a few hours later, the sorrow was still there. Numb with pain, I drove to my social worker's office. Unannounced, I walked in and fell into a chair.

Rachel looked up from her desk. The look she saw on my face reflected absolute devastation.

"Lauren, what's wrong?" Her voice was heavy with concern.

I was too broken to utter a single word. Every time I opened my mouth, a groaning sound came out. It was at least fifteen minutes before I could say anything intelligible. Literal pains stabbed my heart, and I really thought I might die sitting in her office. I had survived a life of tragedy, but I surely could not survive this blow!

At last I quieted down and was able to relate what little I knew about my birth parents. Rachel talked to me for a long while, but her comfort could not reach my pain. I left her office with the agreement that I would hang in there, but I knew that I would never be healed. I was just too broken!

That was two-and-a-half years ago. I'm still here. I'm healing, and I will continue to survive.

"How?" you ask. I answer that question for every broken and hurting person who is reading this book. I will survive, and I will be healed in the hands of the Master Potter, the Lord Jesus, who has been picking up the pieces and lovingly restoring me to wholeness. What I couldn't do—what no one could do—Jesus is doing!

And here, perhaps, is the most important point: *I could do nothing more than place my brokenness in His hands. And that was sufficient!*

I feel for you who believe that you are one step beyond rescue, one step beyond repair. I cry with you. I pray for you. I wait with you. I reassure you that a loving God will reach one step beyond to where you are in your brokenness and gently restore you to wholeness. Jesus says to you:

> I am close to the brokenhearted and I save those who are crushed in spirit (Psalm 34:18 NIV).

The "405"

After ten months of nonstop traveling for radio interviews and television programs, I was becoming weary, not only physically but emotionally, and there seemed to be no stopping place. I was fast learning that either I was not built to be a jet-setter or that jet-setting is not all it's cracked up to be!

Now it was just seven days before Christmas. I knew things had to stop for at least two days! But I had six more TV and radio interviews scheduled before my time off, and they were all on the same day. The Lord was faithful and strengthened me for them. But trying to drive back to my motel during rush-hour traffic on the 405 freeway turned out to be an unexpected trial.

The 405 was crowded—wall-to-wall cars. Once I got on, I immediately wanted to get off! But as it is with most freeways in Southern California, once you are in the fast lane, you *stay* in it!

Cars were whizzing by and dangerously darting in and out in front of me, and horns were honking. Then the unexpected came. Ten months of strain hit me squarely in the face.

Tears that had been choked back for several days began to stream down my face. "God, get me out of here!" I cried. "And hurry!" I thought to myself, *Isn't this an immediate crisis—one that needs Your attention—quickly?*

It sounds almost humorous now, but believe me, at that time I was dead serious.

As I began again to voice my plea to the Lord, I noticed the cassette tape June Hunt had given me after our tapings for her radio program, "Hope for the Heart." I rather perfunctorily put it into my car tape player and pushed the play button.

"Surrendered, surrendered, I'm standing still. I give up, I give up my will to Your will."[1] The words couldn't have been more timely. I didn't want to surrender *anything* at that moment—especially not my will! The last thing I wanted to say was, "Not *my* will, but *Thine* be done." But at that moment, *though my situation didn't change, God began to change me.*

"Okay, God. I'm stuck here, and I need Your help. Whatever You choose to do is all right with me."

"You're not alone, my child. I am with you, and my strength will be sufficient for you. I will take control."

I felt my fingers relax their grip on the steering wheel. I wiped my tears away and heaved a sigh of relief. For it wasn't *my* problem any longer. It was *His* problem.

Hurts Are Hurts and Problems are Problems

In comparison to trials of a greater magnitude, my "405" trial might seem rather minor. But I share it with you because that which may appear to be a *small* problem to outsiders can be a *big* problem to the person going through it. Compared to the horrendous situations I've gone through in past years, this trial should have been a snap to get through. Right? It would seem so.

But believe me, I felt pretty desperate on the 405. Why? Because I was at the end of my rope. And when you are at the end, you are at the end no matter what the trial is!

When I cried, "Help!" God didn't speak to me in a thundering voice saying, "Lauren, what is wrong with you? Can't you even make it through a *little* problem by yourself? Do this one on your own!"

Oh no! We don't serve a God like that! I think that is why many of us don't ask God to help us. We think our problem is too small for Him to bother with. Our hurt is just a *little* hurt. Somewhere along the line, many of us have adopted the erroneous belief that we are only to go to God with *major* problems.

Is that what the Scriptures teach? Did Christ say, "Cast only your *big* cares upon me?" No! Jesus tells us to cast *all* our cares upon Him, for He cares for us.

So when I am feeling trapped and spent with exhaustion on the 405, it is no small matter to my Heavenly Father. *If it is not small to me, it is not small to Him! No matter how big or small our hurt—God cares!*

Many hurting souls who have read *Satan's Underground* have made the remark to me, almost apologetically, "Lauren, after reading about all you went through, I feel like I shouldn't even mention my problems to God."

Some people will even detail my past experiences to prove that their experiences of divorce, depression, fear, problems with children, drug addiction, job failures, and so forth are not worthy of even being mentioned, much less being brought to God in prayer.

I can't begin to tell you how I feel when I'm told that. I always reply, "Please don't compare your hurts with mine. When you're hurting, you're hurting. Your hurt needs attention just as much as mine."

Yes, I've been broken, and I'm not "all well" yet. I'm still healing. I still hurt—not nearly as much as I used to, but nevertheless, I hurt. And new hurts and trials come my way daily. Unfortunately, that's the way life is, and none of us are immune to its crises, whether big or seemingly small.

The good news is: Jesus has promised to be with us! He will minister to us as we surrender our will to His and allow Him to take over, even if it means He has to minister to us in the midst of utter darkness.

A Light in the Darkness

Of course the enemy of our souls would like us to think that if God really cared, we wouldn't hurt—and we surely wouldn't get our faces bloodied in the struggle. Or he gets us to thinking, "I'll show God. I can make it through this one on my own!" Whether the words are said in defiance or in bitterness, they are futile. The enemy will use any reasoning to keep us from allowing God to draw nigh to us in our darkest times.

I don't know how many times I've been asked, "Why didn't you turn against God when horrors kept surrounding you year after year, and every time you turned for help you ran into a brick wall?" They usually add, "I would have gotten so mad at God!"

"I did!" I reassure them. I grew exceedingly angry at times. And, yes, there were times when God and I weren't on very good speaking terms. (My choice only.) But turn against Him? Lock Him out? Never! He was all I had! Those traumatic circumstances required His presence, not His absence.

If you are in a situation that is shattering your world right now, let me ask you a question. Can you go it alone? Well, you can try. But there's a strange thing about darkness. Many POWs have been victims of what is known as "light deprivation." They describe the trauma of being forced to live in total darkness with not even one ray of light. The prisoner of war tries to describe the feeling of aloneness that darkness produces. He tries to recount his inability to tell how long he's been in his darkness as the days and weeks and months begin to multiply.

People in this situation begin to forget what light is like after being surrounded by darkness for so long. They feel as if they are losing their self-identity after being deprived of communication with the outside world. The one who has been in utter darkness says that he has been robbed of his will to live.

So it is with you and me in our hard times. If our darkness is prolonged with no ray of hope in sight, we cannot help but be adversely affected. We become like the POW who is suffering from light deprivation. Our feeling of aloneness in our darkness increases. And after a while, we tend to feel we've been in our dark place forever, instead of the week or the month it's really been. In fact, like the POW, we begin to believe that we will always be in darkness, and no daylight will ever shine in our lives again!

Jesus wants to be our light, our ray of hope. But if we deny Him entrance into our dark place, we will become disoriented, and our ability to think rationally will diminish. Nothing grows in darkness. Without the presence of Jesus, our hope can do nothing but wither and die.

"Just Get Me Out!"

When we feel ourselves being crushed by painful problems, we usually want one of two things. We either want the hurtful situation changed, or we want to be removed from it.

In the midst of almost daily abuse as a child, I used to have fairy-tale fantasies of Jesus swooping down like Superman and rescuing me. Sunday School teachers had taught me that Jesus could do anything. In child-like faith, I knew that He wouldn't want a little girl to be hurt and so scared. I would finally go to sleep by dreaming about Jesus coming right through my bedroom wall, picking me up by some magical power and flying me home to heaven to live with Him.

Only the nature of the fantasy changed as I got older. No Superman, no magical lights, no childlike dreams of fairy-tale rescues. But I never stopped wanting out.

Many adults who were abused as children have asked me, "If God is a loving God, why didn't He rescue me? After all, I was just a defenseless child. I didn't deserve what I had to go through." The bitterness and hurt all but scream from their voices.

- ✦ Women who are living in a devastating marriage.

- ✦ Parents whose rebellious teenagers are making their lives unbearable.

- ✦ Men and women who are barely getting through the days and months, year after year with chronic illnesses.

- ✦ Persons who battle depression that seems to hang in heavy clouds over them.

We all want out! Is this too much to ask of a Father who desires to give us only good gifts? Of a Father who is loving, compassionate and merciful? Surely a loving Father doesn't want us to hurt.

Then where is the rescuing? Where is the healing? Why hasn't it come?

I can only share with you what I've found in the midst of my crushing hurts, in the midst of my darkest hours. It has been a life-changing reality, not a hopped-up slogan that helps me fool myself or tricks me into imagining things are better. God's Word has provided a promise of hope in the midst of all pain:

The Lord has promised to be in the darkness with us!

If He never leaves us or forsakes us, then *where we are, He is*! When He has not chosen to immediately remove us from the pain, or to take the pain from us, He has vowed that He will draw near to us in the midst of our thick darkness. He chooses for us to know Him, not only in His divine providence of mercy, but in the sorrow of our affliction. Though He may not spare us, he promises to be with us.

Why would God choose to minister to me in the midst of my darkness rather than take me out of it? Doesn't that seem a little cruel?

I know only to say that the most meaningful times with the Lord Jesus, those that have drawn me closer to Him, and the most healing times have come in the midst of my pain. And some of the ways God has chosen to bring healing have been both simple and unique.

Raggedy Ann

We all know the famous twin dolls, Raggedy Ann and Raggedy Andy, the stuffed, limp characters dressed in blue and white with the red yarn hair and the red triangle noses. Many of you had Raggedy Ann or Andy to play with as children. I did not. I never owned a doll. So my adult experience with a Raggedy Ann doll was a first.

Raggedy Ann came into my life about five years ago when I was just beginning to deal with the worst abuses of my childhood. She was handmade especially for me by a friend. Nancy had even taken the pains to hand stitch an outline of a red heart with the words, "I LOVE YOU," on the body of the doll where the heart would be. Raggedy Ann is dressed in a blue dress and a darling white pinafore. Underneath the pinafore and dress are the cutest bloomers that come down to her knees. She is a sight to behold! I think all little girls would trade almost anything to own her.

Any girl, that is, but me.

I loved my friend Nancy, and I was overwhelmed at the thought that she had stayed up late several nights making the doll. I remember telling her that she had done such a remarkable job that she could make a fortune in the doll business. Her response was, "No way, Lauren. My heart and soul are in that doll. That's what makes her so special!"

This Raggedy Ann was special all right. No doubt about it. But she scared me to death. I had never even set a doll on my bed for decoration much less held a doll in my arms. To me, dolls represented Lauren Stratford, the frightened, lonely little girl. I wanted no part of them.

I tried. I really tried to overcome my fear. I set Raggedy Ann in my rocking chair in the living room. She was just made for that chair! But every time I looked at her, I saw myself as a little girl, and the pain was too great.

I'm ashamed to admit it, but a few days later I could look at her no more. I stuffed her in a large grocery sack and hid her in the darkest corner of my closet. There she stayed month after month and year after year. Only when I cleaned my closet really well did I get back far enough to reach the sack. Only then did I dare to look inside and peek at her to see if it still hurt.

It did—each time.

But every time I did make the effort to look at her and at least acknowledge the fact that she was there, I was making a small attempt to face the scared and lonely little girl that lived in me. Little did I know that the Lord Jesus was quietly and unobtrusively beginning a healing in the heart of that little girl.

Just as the replica of The Leaning Tower of Pisa was "rediscovered" in my moving, so Raggedy Ann made an encore appearance.

I reached into a sack. My hand came out holding a mop of bright red hair—Raggedy Ann's! My heart gave several extra-hard thumps. My normal instinct was to let go of her, but I didn't. To my surprise, I drew her to myself and held her tight.

It was only for a few seconds, but the length of time wasn't important. What was important was the fact that I held her at all.

I began to put her back in the sack when I thought of the window seat in my bedroom. "Raggedy Ann belongs on that seat," I heard myself say out loud. Equally as surprising, I found myself taking her into my bedroom and setting her on the seat. I stood back and looked at her fully expecting that I would again be filled with fear, and that I would grab her and stuff her into the sack once again.

The Lord had a different plan. "I can leave her there. I can! She's going to be all right," I said emphatically.

Raggedy Ann hasn't moved from her place on the window seat for over three months now! And every morning I look at her and smile, and see that she is smiling back at me.

This healing process—the mending of my own broken pottery—is not my job. I'm just sort of standing back and watching it day by day. I don't understand how the Lord is doing it, but I surely know it is He who is at work. I'm not really doing anything.

I used to think that I had to "get involved" in the process of healing. I used to think that healing always had to be at least a little painful and surely very slow. And I, like most people, thought I had to be out of my hard place before healing could begin.

That's just not so. Jesus can do some dramatic things for us in the darkest corners of our hard places. I'm realizing that more and more. That realization has given me a hope even in my pain.

I'm convinced that Raggedy Ann was Jesus' idea! Who else but Jesus could have come up with a Raggedy Ann to bring hope and healing to a very old and deeply-buried hurt? Who else but Jesus would have given a happy and smiling Raggedy Ann to a sorrowing and frightened adult who had never held a doll in her arms before?

From the Inside Out

The Lord has often chosen to touch me from the inside, not removing, changing or even touching my situation to make it better. Rather, He has touched *me*, working in my heart, working in my spirit, working on my inner being.

Dear one, let me encourage you with this hope. *Though every single outer circumstance should remain unchanged, God will be with you.* When you cry out to Him, "Touch my heart. I'm hurting," His loving hands will reach out to you. When you invite Him into the darkness of your pain, He will be there!

> Your hurt is never too much for God. NEVER!
> When it gets too much for you;
> When the trials are too many;
> When the hurt goes too deep;
> When the darkness is too terrifying;
> When you get to the point of helplessness;
>
> You can be sure of one thing:
> The Master Potter is there with you.
> He is skillful.
> He is tender.
> He is able to put your life together again.

– 3 –

It's Just You and Me, God!

It was Christmas day, 1988, at sunset. I was sitting in my car, alone, looking out over the Pacific Ocean. My doors were locked for safety. I closed my eyes, and leaning my head against the headrest I breathed a sigh of heaviness.

"Dear Jesus, I feel so alone!"

Part of me thought, *That's stupid! You just spent Christmas day in a house filled with people who love you. You have family and friends. And you're feeling alone?*

I smiled faintly at the irony, but the sensation continued. "But I am alone! All alone. It's You and me against the world, God."

In my experience, this sense of isolation is one of the emptiest and loneliest feelings on earth.

I was in the midst of it that Christmas afternoon. Despite countless personal victories, I still have times when my past hits me like a thud in the pit of my stomach, and I need to be by myself to get over it. I've never been one to indulge in self-pity for long periods of time. However, there are still moments when I have one of those "It's You and me against the world" attacks.

To have that feeling for a few minutes is bad enough. But I know very well that there are those who experience it day after day, month after month and perhaps even year after year. Such loneliness is hell on earth! It's a hell that is fueled by bitterness, loss, death, separation, divorce, failure, hurt, resentment, abuse, anger, hatred, disappointment, loneliness, aloneness, despair, devastation, and a host of other emotions.

Who experiences such pain? Strangers with nameless faces? No! I'm talking about you and me. I'm talking about human beings whose hearts have been wounded. Everyday men and women find themselves feeling hopeless, alone, let down, knocked down and left to heal themselves. It's no wonder we cry out, "It's just You and me, God!"

Worse yet, maybe we can only whisper, "It's just me— all alone!"

My heart hurts with you. I grieve over letters I receive from people who have been so hurt that the pain in their words could almost be wrung out in drops like water from a washcloth. Occasionally, I have to walk away from a letter for a few moments, because the writer's pain is so acute that I cannot bear the weight of it in one sitting.

I read letters that relate such sadness, such despair and such tragedy that the writer can only write in conclusion, "Don't tell me to pray. Don't tell me to trust God. If He really loved me, none of this would have happened."

My mail records the bitterness of hopes deferred. The anger of dashed dreams. The despair of unfulfilled lives. The agony of love that has been killed.

How have we become so disillusioned, so cynical and so hopeless? We see a church on every other corner and a Bible in every other home. In North America we live in relative affluence, seeing dreams come true and hearing amazing rags-to-riches stories. Everybody has a chance. Anyone can make it.

So how can it be that hundreds of people are writing to me saying, "I don't have any hope left. Life isn't worth living any longer"? Why is it that I get at least one letter per week that ends with, "I just want to die"?

It's No Wonder...

✦ When perhaps one fourth of our children are sexually abused;

✦ When ritual abuse of our very young children is one of the new crimes of the 1980's;

✦ When one out of every two marriages ends in divorce;

✦ When our children and teenagers are sharing their homes and mothers with different men on a weekly or monthly basis;

✦ When the number of alcoholics and drug addicts, especially among our teenagers, is rising so rapidly that we can only make estimates;

✦ When there is a teenage suicide every thirty minutes in this country;

✦ When girls are trying to live with the consuming guilt of having aborted an unborn child;

✦ When there are more than 20,000 homeless young people living on the streets of New York City and over 12,000 in Los Angeles;

✦ When 38 percent of these youngsters under the age of eighteen, who have been tested for AIDS, have tested positive;

✦ When churches have ceased to preach the true gospel of Jesus Christ—the only gospel that has the power to transform the life destroyed, heal the heart torn apart, turn sorrow into joy, forgive sins and erase guilt, and promises hope of eternal life.

It's no wonder that I receive letters from people who are saying, *"I just want to die!"*

It's no wonder that brokenhearted mothers write about sons whose rooms are filled with satanic writings signed in blood, stating that they've given their souls to Satan, their Master.

It's no wonder that young women write about an incestuous act they've never revealed to another soul.

It's no wonder that grown men write about their enslavement to pornography. Their own fathers left it around the house for them to read as ten-year-olds!

So where is the reason to go on living? Is there hope at the end of the tunnel?

Paulette, Ray, Charlie and Jennifer

Lying on my desk in front of me is a tragic letter from a mother with a daughter and a son—both teenagers. Their names have been changed, but ask anyone who ministers to the hurting and they'll tell you that their story is not a rarity. The tragedy is repeated in hundreds of other families across the country. I'll summarize the story.

The mother, Paulette, married young—too young. Her husband, Ray, was a handsome, athletic-type guy. He liked to drink, but hey, don't all healthy boys in high school drink? Paulette became pregnant, and they decided the only thing to do was to get married.

Things went well for a few months. Then the baby came. Was he ever cute, but did he ever cost a lot more than they had expected! With the added pressures of a second job he had landed to bring in more income, Ray began to drink heavily. Soon his drinking was out of control, and he was fired from both jobs. Ashamed of having to go on welfare and bored from being around the house all day, he began to drink more and more.

Charlie, their infant son, got on Ray's nerves. Paulette came home one day after pounding the pavement for a job (any job!), only to discover Ray being physically abusive to little Charlie.

Paulette was horrified! She and Ray got into a big quarrel which ended violently. Ray beat her up for the first time.

Paulette wanted to leave and go back to her parents, but she couldn't. They had told her if she quit high school to marry Ray, she could forget about ever coming home. "You made your bed, now lie in it!" her father had told her. She would never forget those words.

So Paulette stayed with Ray and soon learned she was pregnant again. The anticipation of a new baby gave Ray a spark of hope. It also produced a string of promises. "Paulette, we're going to start over. I'm going to quit drinking and find a job. You wait and see. I'll make you proud of me." He lowered his head as he added, "And I'll be a good father to little Charlie again." Ray did try. He quit drinking, or at least he drank less, until three job applications were turned down.

Meanwhile a neighbor asked Paulette to go to church with her. She wanted to go. "Maybe the church people can help us," she confided to her new friend. But when she went home and told Ray she was going to the church down the street, he said, "No! You are not going. We don't need anyone but ourselves!"

In a few months, a baby girl was born to Ray and Paulette. Jennifer was a beauty! So tiny. So fragile and helpless. "She needs me, hon," Ray said proudly. "I'm gonna take real good care of her. I won't let her down." They brought Jennifer home to the small apartment. Paulette also brought home new hopes and new promises. But two babies were a whole lot different than one baby! Two babies crying, two sets of diapers, two feeding times and on and on. Ray only knew one way of escape. The bottle. Every frustration became an excuse to drink, and there were plenty of frustrations!

Ray's drinking became almost continuous. The welfare check began to support it. With little money for food and no money for rent, Paulette and Ray had to move in with his family. The nightmare grew worse. Ray's father was an alcoholic also. In one of Ray's all-night drinking sprees, the secret came out. For years it had been like a stick of dynamite waiting to be lit.

Incest.

Ray's father had committed incest with him when he was just ten years old. As the tale was spilled out, Ray began to sob uncontrollably and beat on his father. Horrified, Paulette grabbed the kids and ran outside. Ray stumbled after her.

They began to move from shelter to shelter. Unknown to Paulette, Ray began to sexually abuse Charlie and Jennifer.

The life of Ray and Paulette and Charlie and Jennifer continued on in abuse, drinking, quarrels and beatings. If it had not been for the occasional periods of two to three months of relative calm when Ray would try to get himself together, Paulette would have left him. But she always hung on to the dwindling hope that during one of his "better times," Ray would finally make it.

He didn't. One night he borrowed a neighbor's car and crashed it into a tree. He was killed instantly. Ray became another D.U.I. statistic.

Today Paulette is managing, but barely. She's free now to go to church. Charlie and Jennifer went with her until they turned fourteen and fifteen. Then Paulette heard the words, "We don't want to have anything to do with God." After much discussion, with Paulette trying to get them to tell her why, the horrible truth came out.

"Dad had sex with me. A lot! I thought I was the only one. But Jennifer...Jennifer just told me that Dad made her have sex with him, too!" Charlie blurted the words, and the anger and hate in his voice weighed heavily in the air.

"You talk about God being our Father, Mom. What

kind of 'Father' lets that happen? You tell me!" Charlie shouted.

Paulette was stunned, too stunned to reply. She reached out to take Jennifer and Charlie in her arms, but they backed off. "We love you, Mom," Charlie said, trying to explain, "but Jennifer and I have talked it over."

"Mother," Jennifer interrupted, "how could you let Dad molest us? You must have known. It went on for too long for you to not know at least *something* was going on."

No amount of Paulette's pleading influenced her children to change their feelings. Too much, too awful, too many years. It was too late!

Paulette's last sentence in her letter informed me that Charlie has gotten his girlfriend pregnant and wants to marry her.

Jennifer has isolated herself into her own private world. She refuses to date or socialize with her friends. When she comes home from school, she shuts herself in her bedroom and seldom comes out.

The plea at the end of Paulette's letter echoes the hurt of everyone else in this chapter. "Lauren, there's no one left. I think there's only God, and I'm not even sure about Him anymore!"

What Do I Tell Them?

"It's just You and me, God!" is the cry of hearts who will forever remain nameless.

What am I to write back to the Paulettes of this world? They need answers. They deserve help. I sit with pen and paper feeling so helpless. Sometimes I shed tears. But I know how to pray, and I always pray, regardless of how impossible the situation seems. I ask God for wisdom, for guidance, and for the voice of the Holy Spirit to guide me as I begin to write my response.

To the Paulettes of the world, I would begin by saying that God and you *are* enough! Change the phrase, "It's just You and me, God," to "It's You and me, God!" God really is all you need! When you are in a trial in which everything in your life has been narrowed down to God and you, then you are at the point of total dependency and total abandonment. And that's when He goes to work! He becomes:

your **Advocate**	1 John 2:1
your **Balm in Gilead**	Jeremiah 8:22
your **Beloved**	Matthew 12:18
your **Confidence**	Proverbs 3:26
your **Counselor**	Isaiah 9:6
your **Friend**	Proverbs 18:24
your **Helper**	Hebrews 13:6
your **Hiding Place**	Isaiah 32:2
your **High Priest**	Hebrews 3:1
your **Hope**	Psalm 71:5
your **Keeper**	Psalm 121:5
your **Morning Star**	Revelation 2:28
your **Resting Place**	Jeremiah 50:6
your **Restorer**	Psalm 23:3
your **Rock of Refuge**	Psalm 31:2
your **Surety**	Hebrews 7:22
your ***All in All***	Colossians 3:1

The list of names for Jesus is ten times longer than this. He will become whatever you need!

Please don't feel that I'm "putting you off" onto Jesus; that it's an "easy out" to tell someone all they need is Him. There's no excuse for telling someone in need to go to Jesus just to avoid bothering with them. But the fact is, in the midst of ministering to hundreds of needy souls, I feel privileged for the opportunity of saying it to you. It is true. You *can* make it with God! In fact, I'll go one better than that. You *will* make it with God!

He stretches out His arms to you, waiting for you to run to Him and cling to Him. He says to you:

> I am big enough to be your everything. My heart is big enough to hold your hurt. Let me carry you. Your shoulders are narrow. Mine are wide.

My friend, when you are hidden in God, nothing and no one can steal you from His presence, His protection and His loving care!

Psalm 32:7 says, "You are my hiding place from every storm of life" (TLB). What does this mean? It means that you can run to the safety of Jesus and hide in His arms. Rest your weary head upon His shoulder. Put your hands in His nail-scarred hand. You and He fit together perfectly. You were meant to depend on Him for your everything.

Jesus Is! That is reality! The Gospel of Jesus Christ is truth! That is reality! We're not dreaming. We're not imagining or visualizing. We are standing on a firm foundation—the reality of Jesus Christ and His Word. Listen to what the apostle Paul says about Jesus Christ, the Son of God.

> He always does exactly what he says. He carries out and fulfills all of God's promises, no matter how many of them there are (2 Corinthians 1:19,20 TLB).

What does He promise to you when you're feeling alone, abandoned, forsaken? You can take His Word to Him in prayer and say, "Lord Jesus, this is Your Word. I ask You and I expect You to carry out Your promise to me. I'm believing that You will make it a reality in my life for today."

Your Lifeline

There are two verses that have been my very lifeline in my loneliest times. I offer them to you. Read them slowly. Know that they are God's promises—to you. His promise is not only a legally binding, but a spiritually binding declaration, giving you a right to claim the carrying out of that promise! Think of this first:

> God Himself has said, I will not in any way fail you nor give you up nor leave you without support. [I will] not, [I will] not, [I will] not in any degree leave you helpless nor forsake you nor let [you] down (relax My hold on you)! [Assuredly not!] (Hebrews 13:5 AMP).

And now, consider this:

> Casting the whole of your care [all your anxieties, all your worries, all your concerns, once and for all] on Him, for He cares for you affectionately and cares about you watchfully (1 Peter 5:7 AMP).

In the verses you just read, Jesus says that He cares for you affectionately and watchfully. He is promising that He will not in any way fail you, give you up or leave you. He is telling you that He will not leave you helpless; that He will not forsake you nor let you down. He says that He will support you, never relaxing His hold on you! Assuredly not!

Can you now see why you and God *can* make it? That you and God means you *with* God? That when you cry out, "It's just You and me, God!" it's okay? Your cry need no longer be uttered in *desperation*, but in *declaration*! "I am with God! God is with me! It's safe to walk with God! It's safe to trust His Word!"

Lamentations 3:24 says, "The Lord is my portion . . . therefore will I hope in him" (KJV). A portion is an exact measurement of a necessary ingredient. The Lord is your portion. He is exactly what you need! Not too much. Not too little. Without the Lord Jesus as the necessary portion in your life, you cannot be a whole person. It takes the two of you together, He in you and you in Him, to make you complete. When you are complete, even though no one else is around, you are all right! You are sufficient in Him!

There will be times when you take two steps forward in trusting God only to find yourself taking one step backward. The feeling of aloneness can creep up at the most unsuspecting moment. The enemy often comes in through the back door, silently and unnoticed, until suddenly he is right in your face exclaiming gleefully, "Surprise! Surprise! I'm here!" The important thing to remember in those times is that the enemy does not have the right to take over!

Christmas Day Again

I began this chapter sitting in my car overlooking the Pacific Ocean. It was Christmas day, and I was feeling very alone. It was tempting, believe me, to give in to Satan's sudden and unexpected attack. Once in awhile, I still do take a step backward and listen to the enemy's voice. But that afternoon I didn't.

I was watching the beauty of the sun, so round and full as it was slipping silently behind the ocean and beyond. I began to feel insignificant and small, too small for the Lord to know I even existed. After telling Him how alone I was feeling, I added, "Who am I, Lord? Who am I that You would be mindful of me?"

The Lord was gracious to answer, and I heard His response deep in my soul. "My child, yes, I have made the vast expanses of the ocean. I have made that great, brilliant, orange ball of fire, the sun. I have made the waves that roll endlessly onto the shore. I have made the broad reaches of sky. I have made the golden rays of the sun that you see reflecting against the clouds. Yes, I created it all! But I also created you, and I see you! You matter to me!

"I see you there in your car. I love you. You can't hide from me. You're not too insignificant for me. You are more important than the magnificent creation of the sun. You are more important than all of the vast expanses of the ocean. You are more important than the beauty of the blue sky above you.

"Let me tell you, my beloved, why you are more important than anything else I've created. It's because you commune with me, and you let me commune with you. I can walk with you. I can put my arms around you and comfort you. That's why you matter to me. Oh my little one, don't ever feel insignificant. Remember how much I love you? I died for you. And one day you're going to reign with me."

Wow! I was so blessed and so comforted and so encouraged that I hadn't even noticed that the sun had slipped behind the horizon, and it was getting dark. I felt warm and whole inside. I felt important to God!

For the first time in my life, I realized that God longs for me just as I long for Him.

"God, I'll walk with You," I whispered. "I'll talk with You. I'll be Your friend." And then, in a triumphant voice of rejoicing, I exclaimed, "God, You not only matter to me, I matter to You!" Tears filled my eyes. Not of sadness, but tears from a heart of joy.

The Lord brought the words of a verse to my mind. I took my little New Testament (with Psalms and Proverbs added) out of the glove compartment and thumbed through the Psalms until I found it. I read:

When I consider your heavens, the work of
your fingers, the moon and the stars, which
you have set in place, what is man that you are
mindful of him, the son of man that you care
for him? (Psalm 8:3,4 NIV).

I closed the New Testament and prayed just one sentence. "I know, Lord, who I am."
My prayer for you is that you, too, will know who you
are in Christ Jesus.

Designed by God

Do you know that you are more important to your
Heavenly Father than everything else He's created put
together? Do you know that you matter to Him? Do you
know that you were especially designed by Him? He's
continually reminding us that it is He who made us, and
we are His.

You made all the delicate, inner parts of my
body, and knit them together in my mother's
womb. Thank you for making me so wonder-
fully complex! It is amazing to think about.
Your workmanship is marvelous—and how
well I know it.

You were there while I was being formed in
utter seclusion! You saw me before I was born
and scheduled each day of my life before I
began to breathe. Every day was recorded in
your Book!

How precious it is, Lord, to realize that you
are thinking about me constantly! I can't even
count how many times a day your thoughts
turn towards me. And when I waken in the

morning, you are still thinking of me! (Psalm
139:13-18 TLB).

Who else can say of us, "I knew you before you were
even conceived; I knew you in your mother's womb; I
know you now; and I've scheduled every day of your life
since before you took your first breath"?

All I can say is, "How I thank You, Lord!"

Every day is provided to us with His knowledge, is
allowed by Him, and comes to us with His stamp of
approval. The Lord made you. He knows every step you
take. And He will not forget to help you.

I urge you to know who you are in Him.

You are not a mistake.
You are not man's idea.
You are God's idea,
    a special creation, designed by God!

And if you feel alone, believe me, you are not.
He is with you.

And He is enough!

– 4 –

I Wait with You

◆

Do you like waiting? I certainly don't. I have never liked waiting anywhere for anything. Grocery stores. Post offices. Restaurants. Gas stations. They all have lines, and they're all my enemies.

With the permission of my dear friend, Joyce Landorf Heatherley, I'm going to borrow three words from her writings, because those of us who are still hurting from yet unhealed wounds are waiting in a somewhat different way. We are delayed in a place Joyce has called "God's Waiting Room." We feel as though we're caught in a holding pattern. We're not going in either direction. We're just there, and more often than not, "there" is where we don't want to be!

My friend Carmen and I were about to leave New York, heading home together. Our flight schedule included a connecting flight, and I couldn't help but think, *It'll be a miracle if we make our connection.* Since this was Carmen's first airplane experience, I didn't want to dampen her excitement. I kept my doubts to myself.

As the plane pulled away from the passenger ramp on schedule, I heaved a sigh of relief and smiled to myself. *Maybe we'll make it after all.* Within a few minutes, the stewardess had taken our dinner order for Chateaubriand with béarnaise sauce.

We got ready to relax and enjoy ourselves.

I don't remember having prayed for patience that morning, but I must have! Suddenly the plane stopped. No movement. No engine sound. And no air-conditioning! "Oh well," I mused, trying to be positive. "Just a minor delay. I think we have two or three minutes to spare."

Five minutes passed. Then 15, 20, 30 minutes! I turned to Carmen. "We've missed the last connecting flight home," I sputtered. "What are we going to do?" Little did I know that God was quietly ushering me into His waiting room.

A calm, cool, collected voice came over the intercom. "Ladies and gentlemen. This is your captain speaking."

Here comes the bad news, I thought. Was I ever right! "The plane is sitting on the tarmac," the voice continued. "We are experiencing a slight delay. Our engines won't start. But there's nothing to get concerned about."

"Nothing to get concerned about? Sure! Anything you say, Mr. Captain," I muttered under my breath.

Then came the clincher. Again the captain's voice. "A truck will be along shortly, and a mechanic will climb a ladder to start the engines manually." And another reassurance of, "There's nothing to be concerned about."

"Who's kidding whom? I'm no dummy!" I grumbled. "Carmen, what if the engines go out again while we're 20,000 feet in the air? Is the mechanic going to ride along and restart them up there?"

Poor Carmen! Her first flight, and I sure wasn't making her day!

One hour passed. Two hours. Still no air. "No, the doors can't be opened." "No, we can't show a movie." *If this lasts much longer*, I thought, *the announcement is going to be, "No, sorry, you can't breathe!"*

Three hours! Talk about a waiting room! Talk about standing in a holding pattern, not going in either direction. Talk about being where one doesn't want to be. Ask me if I was pleased!

As it turned out, our wait lasted for five hours. The trip home took all of twelve hours from start to finish. We could have crossed the entire country three times!

Did I learn anything about patience in all that time? Believe it or not, I did. I really did. For one thing, I discovered that for all my huffing and puffing, it got me nowhere. It only wore me out! When I finally grew weary enough of my straining against the inevitable, I sat back in my seat, took a deep breath and said, "It's in your hands, captain. I can't start the engines for you."

No sooner had I given it back to the captain (as if I could have done anything about it anyway!), then I was content to wait.

Not overjoyed, but content. I had to talk myself into doing it, but I actually relaxed, knowing that we weren't going anywhere for a long while, and there was absolutely nothing I could do about it. It really had been in the captain's hands all along, no matter how I felt or acted.

My waiting room was hot. My seat was uncomfortable. And I really would have liked to have been anywhere but there! Nevertheless, I *was* there, and I had to remain there until the captain decided it was safe to resume the flight.

But It Hurts to Wait!

God's waiting room is seldom, if ever, an easy place in which to be. It is rarely pleasant. We who hurt and are waiting to be healed go through a host of emotions.

- ✦ Why do I have to wait?
- ✦ Why isn't God doing anything?
- ✦ How long do I have to wait?
- ✦ Will my waiting ever end?

When we are in the waiting room, we often feel as if

God has chosen to pass us by. We see our friends delivered. We hear other people's shouts of victory. Someone else we know may have been waiting for only a day or two. We have been waiting forever (or so it seems)! How often have we complained bitterly, "God, where are You? Have You forgotten about me?"

We see nothing. We hear nothing. We feel nothing. And we begin to doubt everything—especially the wisdom of God!

Those sentences describe my waits to a tee. In the times of waiting throughout my life, situations only worsened. Sometimes there was no door, and I could do nothing but wait. Other times, there seemed to be a door, and I tried to get out, but to no avail. I was pushed back in. I didn't see or feel God working, and there were times when even His voice remained silent.

I heard the taunts of my enemies echoing those of David's when they scoffingly asked, "Where is that God of yours?" (Psalm 42:10 TLB).

Year after year passed while I sat. I didn't know *why* I was waiting. I didn't know *for what* I was waiting, and I didn't know for *how long* I was going to have to be patient.

I'm continually asked by people who have heard or read my life story, "How did you ever endure those years?"

After a few more questions of that nature, their final comments often are, "You should either be dead, or you should be in a mental institution by now."

Those are valid observations. How does one exist in a furnace of affliction?

One thing I know for certain. If it was true that God was not waiting with me, if He had not been tending to my cries, if He was not accomplishing a work in me while I was waiting, I would have most probably committed suicide or ended up insane.

I encourage you, dear tarrying souls, with these truths.

✦ God has not forsaken you.
✦ God has a purpose in your waiting.
✦ God is effecting that purpose in your life.
✦ God will bring you out!

That I am alive and sane today is testimony to the fact that God did not forsake me in my waiting room; that God had a purpose for my being there. He *was* working out that purpose, and He *did* bring me out in His time.

What Is the Purpose?

God is never doing nothing. Even in your waiting room, something is happening. God never asks you to wait to just get rid of time. He has a plan and an objective for every minute of your life. He has a reason for everything He asks of you. When the word "wait" is spoken, He speaks it in divine wisdom in accordance with a specific purpose. Your obeying His request to wait allows that purpose to be fulfilled.

More often than not, the steps we take in life are only revealed one step at a time. The purpose and plan that God is working out within you as you wait is often a mystery.

Because of our ignorance, it's a temptation to think that God is toying with us; that He has us there just to watch us sweat it out; that He dangles promises of deliverance that are just out of our reach as He cruelly taunts, "Not yet. Not yet."

If God did indeed have a purpose for my waiting room, a room that was filled with abuse and fear and horrors beyond description, what in the world was it? What kind of God do we serve? How could He be a God of love and allow one of His children to wait year after year in that kind of hell?

In the midst of my personal tragedies, I was able to see nothing of what God was doing at that time and nothing of the future—not even a glimpse. He didn't give me a book to read while I was waiting titled, *The Outcome of Lauren Stratford's Life*. I was simply asked to wait. Period.

When I screamed to get out, the answer was always, "Not yet, my child."

But God was carrying out a very special and miraculous work in my life that has only been unveiled to me within the past few years. As each new month passes, God's handiwork, performed in the waiting room, becomes clearer and clearer.

With each letter I receive from a wounded victim that reads, "Thank you for sharing your life. Now I know there's hope for me," I see another reason for my waiting room.

With each letter I receive from a parent who writes, "My son was getting into satanism with some of his friends. I knew it was dangerous, but he wouldn't listen to me. I gave him your book. He stayed up all night reading it, and this morning he gave his heart to Jesus," I see another reason for my waiting room.

With each hurting woman who confides that she was abused sexually as a child, but until she heard me talk so openly and candidly about my abuse she refused to admit it, I see another reason for my waiting room.

On and on the purposes unfold. With each new face and each new story, I fall to my knees in my private place of prayer and whisper, "Thank You, Father, for my waiting room."

I cannot begin to remember all of the hurting Christians who have said, "Thank God you had the courage to admit that, even though you asked Jesus to come into your heart as a child, bad things—*really* bad things—

happened to you! I thought I was the only Christian who went through so many awful things."

Sometimes they confess, "I didn't know of another Christian who was so sorely and continually attacked by Satan. Now I don't feel as guilt-ridden and unforgivable as before."

Again the prayer goes up, "Thank You for my waiting room."

Even in the evilness of the years, God was snatching the plans of Satan from his grimy hands, transforming them into a ministry that would be used twenty years later to help others who are in the same horrifying circumstances.

Who would ever have guessed the blessing that was ahead as Jesus was forging me in the heat of my fiery trial? Surely, not I!

Even when your waiting room seems to have been created and inhabited by Satan himself, God will defeat Satan's designs for your life. Satan's schemes of destruction can be the blueprints for miracles (more about that later!) when put into the hands of the Lord Jesus. And not only is our God working out a wonderful plan for us in this life, He is preparing us for eternity when we will rule and reign with Him.

But bear this in mind. Since the waiting room is not a place you can elect to avoid, the choices you make as to how you will spend your time in it are crucial. You can wait in expectation, or you can wait in despair. You can look forward to the finished product, or you can focus on your present situation. And if your wait is a long one, the wrong choice can make your waiting almost unbearable.

God, What Time Are You On?

If there is one thing I have learned all too well about myself, it's the fact that *my* timetable is seldom the same as God's! I would guess that those of you who are reading this are not much different than me! Human beings do not like to wait. We want things done now!

God's perspective couldn't be more different than ours. He works in a time zone that's neither Pacific, Mountain, Central nor Greenwich Mean. God's time is eternal. It is of infinite duration.

If you're like me, you aren't comfortable with plans that are of an infinite duration. In fact, you probably don't like them at all!

If I have to be "on hold," I want to know for how long. As soon as I sense that I'm being put in another waiting room, I ask God right up front, "God, is this going to last for one hour, one day or one week?" If I have a sneaky suspicion that it's going to be longer than a week, or worse yet, for an unknown amount of time, forget it! I can't handle that.

We want our problems solved yesterday. God may say, "Tomorrow." We want the answers now. God says, "Wait." We want every loose end tied up by the end of the year. God says, "Next year."

Let's remember that whatever God's timetable is, and however long our waiting room experience lasts, it isn't to tease us or to make us squirm and struggle. God doesn't work that way. It may not even be to test you—to see if you have what it takes. God, in His infinite wisdom, simply knows what is best for us.

I can look back now and see that in God's timing, He absolutely knew what He was doing. One of my waiting rooms lasted for over thirty years. His timing was perfect to the very month!

The things that happened so quickly after I got out, one right after another, would not have been possible if my waiting room experience had ended even one year sooner. Even in the timing of the release of *Satan's Underground*, the subject matter of the book would not have had the same acceptance or impact had it been released at an earlier time.

During all those years, when God was looking at the finished product, but I was only seeing my circumstances from moment to moment, I was crying out, "I want out now!" And all God replied was, "Not now. Wait." At the time, I felt His "Not now" was a sort of punishment. It hurts to hurt. It's hard to wait for one year, let alone for several years. But I can now see that God was in my waiting room. We stayed there together until His work of fashioning me into a servant of ministry was completed.

God's purposes do not begin after our waiting room experiences are over, but during. Our Heavenly Father does not sit around, biding His time and yawning, until He can finally say, "Yes, you may come out. Now I can get to work!"

Ecclesiastes 3:1 tells us, "To every thing there is a season, and a time to every purpose..." (KJV). In other words, there is a right time for everything. Even the seasons of waiting have a purpose. The contrariness of our waiting room experiences is equal to the beauty of the finished work. They do not contradict each other. Rather, they embrace and enhance each other!

Ecclesiastes 3:1-8 (NIV) lists some of life's great experiences. "A time to be born and a time to die...a time to weep and a time to laugh, a time to mourn and a time to dance...a time to tear and a time to mend," and so forth.

Exactly half of these times are experiences most of us would call "experiences of the *wrong kind* and of the *wrong time.*"

But the Scripture says that there is a *right time* for *all things*. Each has its own purpose, even times of hurt. The gem of truth, albeit a most difficult one to learn, is that only you can allow those unwanted and uncomfortable times to blossom forth into beauty in your life.

Blossoms in Waiting

Your extraordinary and unbearable affliction will unfold the blossom of God's extraordinary grace.

Your extraordinary inability to deal with your trial will unfold the blossom of God's extraordinary help.

Your extraordinary sorrow will unfold the blossom of God's extraordinary comfort.

Your extraordinary desire to give up will unfold the blossom of God's grace to help you endure.

Your extraordinary feeling of aloneness will unfold the blossom of God's abiding presence.

In your extraordinary waiting room, you will find an extraordinary God!

I encourage you to take heart! While your Father is whispering, "Not now. Not yet. Wait," and you are spending your days in God's waiting room, I encourage you to color your room with blossoms of hope.

> For in your darkness,
>   He has promised to be your light.
> For out of the stillness,
>   He has promised to bring abundant life.
> For though you cannot see the Father
> working,
>   He has promised to finish the work He
>   has begun.
> For though the wait may be long,
>   It will not be forever!
> He will bring you out!
> And until that time comes, dear one,
> He says, "I wait with you."

– 5 –

Intimacy with God

$\blacklozenge$

"I wouldn't trade one sorrow in my life if it meant I wouldn't know Jesus in the intimate way I know Him now."

Often, my audience reacts in amazement and even doubt to these words. It's as if they're thinking, "Come on now. You can't mean that."

But I do mean it. In my darkest hours, I've found Jesus to be my everything, my all in all. I don't say that boastfully. Rather I say it in all humbleness and with thanksgiving in my heart to the Lord who has literally become the provider of my every need.

After the statement that has the audience wondering what in the world I'm talking about, I continue. "Throughout the tragic circumstances of my life, I've found an intimate relationship with the Savior of my soul that I never could have known if it had not been for my very need of Jesus. I had to have Jesus. There were no ifs, ands or buts about it! I could not and would not have survived without Him."

I often sense that my listeners are still experiencing a measure of doubt. And I can't blame them. I would react the same way. Someone who has lived through sexual abuse, pornography, the loss of three children, one of them sacrificed in a satanic ritual—this woman is trying to make us believe that she wouldn't trade any of those hideous experiences? Can she be saying she is actually thankful for them?

No, I'm not thankful for any of my hurts. I'm not thankful for the pain and sorrow. But I am thankful for the relationship I now have in Christ Jesus *because* of those sorrows. My deepest hurts and my darkest hours literally drove me to Him.

I had to have Jesus as my strength, for my own little bit of energy had long been spent. I had to find Jesus as my protector. I surely could not protect myself. Jesus became my healer in the midst of sickness; my peace in turmoil; my mother and father in the absence of loving parents; my hope in hopelessness; and my life when my own physical existence might well have ended.

Will the Yeast Rise?

I did a radio interview on WBRI in Indianapolis, and Kathy Nikou, the host of the program, was most gracious. I had been on an extended tour in several states for ABC television and radio stations. I was looking forward to working with a Christian who would allow me the privilege of ministering the love of Jesus to hurting people.

The secular media leans toward sensationalism—especially regarding the highly-charged subject of satanism and ritualistic abuse. In that setting, there are few opportunities to tell about what Jesus has done for me. So it was with relief and anticipation that I settled myself in front of the microphone.

Kathy was sitting just a few feet away. She had done her research well. What a joy! Most interviewers had not taken the time to read *Satan's Underground* before interviewing me. Kathy's questions were good ones, and got right to the point. She skirted no issue that needed to be addressed. Some queries were difficult to ask and painful to answer, but necessary, nevertheless.

What took place during the back-to-back questions was a first for me and obviously a first for Kathy! The inquiries soon got right down to the nitty-gritty. As I delved into the horrors of sexual and ritualistic abuse, Kathy began to shake her head and close her eyes. After a few more questions and answers, she lowered her head and put her hands over her ears.

It was initially frustrating to me because I thought that the interview wasn't going well and her physical responses were her way of communicating her displeasure. However, it didn't take long for me to figure out that she was having an extraordinarily difficult time in handling the subject matter.

I knew she had made it through the book. I knew she had spent hours of preparation for the interview. Yet here she was, still so overwhelmed that she could barely survive our one hour together.

There were times in responding face-to-face with her that her pain became my pain, and I could barely continue. There were other times that the expressions on her face almost made me laugh. That was a first. I had never been tempted to laugh during an interview before! I finally had to quit looking at her.

We did make it through, and in listening to the tapes of the interview a few weeks later, I sensed a precious ministering of the Lord.

As Kathy drove me to the airport from the radio station, I finally mustered up the nerve to ask her what she had been feeling during the interview.

"Lauren, words can't describe what I went through as you were telling your story," she began. I could tell that it was still affecting her. "You see, I can't relate to a thing you talked about."

I quietly thought, "I can handle that. Most people haven't had to go through such horrors." But I wasn't prepared for Kathy's next revelation. Never had I heard another soul on earth duplicate her words.

"My childhood was perfect. I had two wonderful parents who raised me with much love. We lived in the proverbial house with the white picket fence. I knew no sadness. I've not even had to deal with the death of an immediate family member."

As she continued, I kept thinking, *Wow, that's the kind of childhood I've only dreamed of.* Before my emotional healing, I used to become resentful when someone would describe such a neat childhood. Now I could listen to a person like Kathy and be thankful for the child who didn't know abuse.

Kathy continued. "I married right after I graduated from high school. My husband is a wonderful Christian man who has been very good to me. Now we have two precious little boys who are the joy of our lives." I have to be truthful in admitting that at this point I was becoming a little jealous.

Kathy's final sentence sounded like it came right out a fairy-tale book.

"Lauren, the biggest problem in my life right now is worrying whether the yeast will rise when I'm baking bread."

"You've got to be kidding!" The words blurted out before I could stop them. I was stunned! Why, no one, absolutely *no one* has *that* good of a life! And yet, as I recalled Kathy's reactions during our radio interview, I knew that she was sincere.

Several months later I received a letter from her. She wrote, "I really mean it when I say I ache for you, and the many little kids who are in similar circumstances. Perhaps I feel especially badly because mine was such a happy and productive childhood."

Kathy's next sentence sums up the message of this chapter. "You have insights into the human spirit that someone like me can only imagine!"

Forged in the Heat

I'm not so sure about my insights into the human

spirit. But during our drive toward the airport I began to think about what my relationship with Jesus was and how it quite literally had been forged into a close intimacy in the heat of my pain. I know a love that not only has touched the surface of my heart, but a love that has touched the hurt deep within my heart.

I have an intimacy with Jesus, not *in spite* of hurt, of trials, or of disappointments. My intimacy with Jesus is there *because* of them! That closeness came as a direct result of my pain.

On the plane trip home, I settled back into my seat as comfortably as I could, and I began to reflect on the times I had felt the closest to Jesus. Had they been in the good times, the fairly smooth times, when my days were falling into a "normal" pattern?

Had I felt the closest to Jesus on the mornings that I awakened and was actually able to greet the day with anticipation?

No! Not that I didn't long for those times, for they were few and far between. But the memories that the Lord brought to mind were of the hard times, the unwanted times, the most painful times.

Those were the hours when I found out just how much Jesus really did love me and how much I really did love Him. And those were the moments when my intimacy with Him grew the deepest and strongest.

I remembered in particular the times, too many to count, when I felt not just lonely, but totally alone. Falling to my knees in the darkness of the night, I would weep with an intensity that shook my body.

"Jesus, You're all I have. I need You now! Please put Your arms around me and hold me tight."

I can honestly say that in those most desperate of times, never once did Jesus fail to respond to my cry, drawing me unto Himself, gently bathing me in His love. And oftentimes, as I crawled back into bed, I would feel that I knew Jesus in a way no one else in the whole wide world knew Him. And that was enough—to have experienced His love in the tenderest possible way.

Do you know Jesus as your intimate friend? Do you know Him as the love of your life, of your heart, soul and mind? Have you allowed Him to touch your hurts with His healing? Or have you pushed Him away? Have you built a wall made of the bricks of your pain, trials and bitterness that has denied any possibility of a closeness with Jesus? Has that wall blocked the floodgates of His love from reaching your hurts?

We all have a strong tendency to run *from* Jesus rather than to run *to* Him when periods of trials enter our lives. There's an inclination to avoid communication with God rather than praying all the more. We blame God for our pain rather than going to Him as our sustainer in the midst of it. We often go to every other source we can think of for help. Yet, to the very one who longs to be "a friend who sticks closer than a brother" (Proverbs 18:24 NIV), we slam the door.

I think we've all done that, and probably more often than we care to admit. Let's be honest. When we're hurting, it's only human to want to blame someone else for that hurt. And not only to blame someone else, but to get back at someone, to make him pay, to get revenge. Perhaps we're afraid to confront the person who has hurt us. Perhaps our situation involves too many of the "bad guys" out there. Sometimes we have been our own worst enemy, and we've gotten ourselves into the problem. For whatever reason, it's just a whole lot easier to get mad at God!

God knows. He understands. He doesn't strike us dead when we blame Him. More importantly, He doesn't shut the door to His love just because we've shut the door to our hearts. Thank God for His mercy and patience. Thank God He doesn't yell back at us, "Go ahead and pout. Be stubborn. See if I care. If you don't want my love, that's just fine with me!"

Our Heavenly Father waits patiently for us to come to Him. He longs for us to find in Him an intimate hiding place of refuge. He longs to cover us with His wings. He yearns for us to rest our heads upon His bosom.

True intimacy with Jesus is closeness with Him during times of trouble.

"But 'God' and 'Intimacy' Don't Go Together!"

The word "intimate" and the word "God" might not seem exactly compatible to some people's way of thinking. To be intimate means to be close—very close. Yet the word "God" is intimidating, almost threatening to some people. They have carried the Bible's admonishment to "fear God" to the limit.

How many victims of deep wounding have told me that they imagine God to be this untouchable, unreachable being...out there...somewhere. Many of them picture Him holding a huge bat! His sole purpose for existing is to clobber them when they get out of line!

And we who counsel hurting persons wonder why they have a difficult time getting to know God as their healer!

I considered changing the name of this chapter to "Intimacy with Jesus." And yet I think those of us who need to feel His healing touch on our lives must know the one God—Father, Son, and Holy Spirit. It is theologically impossible to feel close to Jesus and be scared to death of God at the same time.

Those of us who feel intimidated or threatened by God should remember the most well-known verse in the Bible:

For God so loved the world, that he gave his only begotten Son, that whosoever believeth in

him should not perish, but have everlasting
life (John 3:16 KJV).

It was God who loved the world. Not only did He love
the world, but He *so* loved the world. We all know that
Jesus died for us, but we often tend to forget that it was
God who loved us so much that He sent His Son, Jesus,
to die on a cross for us.

I can trust someone who gave His only Son for me. I
can trust someone who took an oath that He would
honor His promises. The Bible talks about why we can
trust God. It's found in Hebrews 6:16-19 and it says:

> When a man takes an oath, he is calling
> upon someone greater than himself to force
> him to do what he has promised. . . . God also
> bound himself with an oath, so that those he
> promised to help would be perfectly sure and
> never need to wonder whether he might change
> his plans.
>
> He has given us both his promise and his
> oath, two things we can completely count on,
> for it is impossible for God to tell a lie. Now all
> those who flee to him to save them can take
> new courage when they hear such assurances
> from God; now they can know without doubt
> that he will give them the salvation he has
> promised them.
>
> This certain hope of being saved is a strong
> and trustworthy anchor for our souls . . . (TLB).

I'll never forget a comment an evangelist made in a
sermon. His words have remained with me for many
years. He was commenting on the verse in Psalms that
says, ". . . your promises are backed by all the honor of
your name" (138:2 TLB).

The preacher said, "Those are the words of a gentleman and back where I come from, the word of a gentleman can be trusted."

Ever since I heard that evangelist refer to the promises of God as "the words of a gentleman," I've thought about how God's honor is at stake when He tells me something. He's putting His reputation on the line when He says, "Come unto me, all ye that labour and are heavy laden, and I will give you rest" (Matthew 11:28 KJV).

When He says, "And the peace of God, which passeth all understanding, shall keep your hearts and minds through Christ Jesus," He's making a promise to me that He will give me peace sufficient to keep me.[1]

He's bound Himself to keeping those promises by taking an oath so we can know, beyond any doubt, that His Word can be trusted.

"Well," you might say, "God can promise all He wants, but that doesn't make me feel any better about trusting Him. And if I'm not sure I can trust Him, I sure don't want to get close to Him!"

You are right. I wouldn't want a best friend I couldn't trust. But how do I discern whether I can trust someone? Let me ask that of you. How do you go about getting close enough to someone to trust them? I'll tell you what I do.

I find out their name. I introduce myself. We chat together. Just small talk. We visit each other. I see how they live and I find out what they like and don't like. We talk on the phone. We go out to eat, and I share a few small things with them. And we spend more and more time together. I begin to share some of my hurts. Our closeness just sort of "happens" over a period of time.

My friendship has been developed through one means—communication. And a closeness with Jesus, a trust in Him, grows through walking with Him and talking with Him.

I never leave Jesus behind. He goes with me everywhere. During the months of writing books, except for an occasional interruption of something I can't get out of, my only traveling away from the house is my daily drive to the post office to get my mail. (Now you know about the exciting life of an author!)

I not only look forward to the "trip" because it gives me a legitimate excuse to get away from the four walls of my study, but I look forward to it because I am alone in my car and I can shut the rest of the world out and talk with God. No fancy talk, rest assured! Sometimes I say nothing. I just think about Him.

Every day that I get in my car and spend that time with Jesus, I get to know Him a little better. And I allow Him to draw a little closer to me. We are not talking about a big production here. We are just talking about my Heavenly Father and me spending time together. That's how I get to know Jesus. And little by little, that's how I come to trust Him. I get to know Him in simple ways, just being with Him.

I had the joy of spending a few days in the mountains last year. I had a room to myself that had large glass windows overlooking a porch. Beyond the porch were tall evergreen trees that reached toward the blue sky.

I was really exhausted. Those three days were the first I had had to myself in over a year. I had come to the retreat to speak, yes. But I had also come to listen and be ministered to. The women were so kind, letting me just be me.

Wearing my jeans and sweatshirt, I sank down into one of the chairs that overlooked the patio. It felt good to relax. I had opened the sliding glass door just a crack, and the smell of green trees and mountain air filled the room. I took a deep breath and shut my eyes. "Thank You, Jesus, for giving this time to me," I whispered.

Suddenly, the quiet was broken by an unfamiliar chattering sound. I opened my eyes and right in front of me on the railing of the porch was a squirrel. He was sitting up on his hind feet just looking at me.

"Oh, Jesus, You've made such beautiful..."

Before I could get the word "creatures" out, I heard a loud, shrill sound. I looked out beyond the porch. On one of the large boughs of an evergreen tree was the most gorgeous bird with a striking blue chest.

"God, You're so good to me. Thank You for sending me these special little animals!"

They were only there for two or three minutes. But in those minutes, I felt so close to God. He had created everything that I was beholding, and His creations were magnificent!

Perhaps the squirrel and bird would have been there whether I was or not. But Jesus ministered to me through them. They were a part of His creation, and caused me to be simply overwhelmed with His beauty and His love. In those few minutes, I got to know Jesus better. I felt like He had drawn closer to me and I to Him.

It is not difficult for me to trust a Heavenly Father who is the creator of such awesome works of nature. That's how I get to know Jesus. In the simplest of ways.

We are best friends. I spend time with Him. I walk with Him in the everyday parts of my life. He's a part of me in everything I do. He's not "up there... somewhere." He's down here right beside me. I don't just set aside special times to talk with Him. We're always talking to each other, and He's always with me.

One day a man said to me, "I wish I could say I knew the man upstairs as well as you. But I'm afraid we're pretty much strangers to each other."

Pretty much strangers! How sad, when it's so easy to know Jesus. I can think of no one I'd rather spend time with than Him. I can tell Him anything. He never breaks my confidence. I can confess my sins to Him. He has always been faithful to forgive me. When I don't know what decision to make, I can go to Him. He guides me through prayer, through just listening to Him speak to my heart, and through reading His Word.

Sometimes when I'm weary or sad or frustrated, I just close my eyes and say, "Jesus." He knows what I'm saying even though I am not expressing it in sentences.

You Can Know Him, Too!

May I say it again? You can know Him, too! Just as easily as I know Him. Just as simply as I know Him. In your everyday life. Wherever you are. Whatever you're doing. You can walk with Jesus. You can be friends. You can share with Him. And you can trust Him.

The first thing you will want to do (if you haven't already done so) is to ask Him to forgive your sins, and invite Him to live in your heart.

Then just tell Jesus you want to get to know Him. If you're scared, tell Him. If you're not sure just how to talk to Him, tell Him that, too. Communicate with Him how you feel. If you want to know Him better, He'll show you how.

And in the meantime....

> Read His Word every day (because that is a primary way He talks to us and we learn what He is like).
>
> Think about Him. Keep Him in your thoughts throughout the day wherever you are. Some people call this "practicing the presence of God."
>
> Talk to Him throughout the day, in simple and short prayers, maybe even just in a sentence or two.
>
> Thank Him for the things you have.
>
> Listen for His quiet, gentle whisper to your heart.

Take the time to notice the beautiful things
He's created in nature and see how lovingly
He must have made each one.

If you will do just simple and common things like that,
you will come to know the God that I know:

a loving,
    a gentle,
        a kind,
            a compassionate,
                a giving,
                    and a caring Savior.

And I will make a promise to you. It will be safe for you
to trust Jesus. I don't make many promises, but I have
no hesitancy in making this one. If you're still a little
unsure of yourself, we're going to talk about that next.
I'm just going to ask that the Lord Jesus will do something special for you that will let you see Him as He
really is—your loving Heavenly Father who longs to
walk with you in your everyday life.

Is Intimacy Too Scary for You?

To those of you who have been wounded or let down by
someone you once trusted, intimacy can be a very frightening proposition.

"I'll never get close to another person in my life!"
Have you ever said that? I've said it, not only once, but
several times. And I meant it! I've heard it from countless others who have been hurt. A heart that has been
injured by arrows shot from another's bow is often understandably wary of trusting, much less of closeness.

For the person who has been physically or sexually
abused, it is even more threatening to risk intimacy,

especially if that intimacy is with someone of the male sex. As the Bible refers to God as "He" and God's Son took on the form of a man when He came to earth, many abused persons have a difficult time of even relating to God the Father and to Jesus, His Son. To call God "My Heavenly Father," or to think of Jesus as "My Savior who is loving, kind and gentle," often requires a deep emotional healing. Many persons, both women and men, who have been sexually abused by their fathers or stepfathers, are unable to accept God as their Father.

Satan delights in robbing the deeply hurt and abused of the comfort and healing that can only be found in Jesus Christ. He has done his work well when he has planted seeds of distrust, fear and even repulsion and hatred in the heart of a hurting soul who is in desperate need of the Father's healing touch.

I read evidence of the enemy's work in the letters I receive almost daily from victims of physical and sexual abuse, as well as from victims of parental divorce. These individuals feel their fathers abandoned them. They vow "I'll never trust or get close to another man again!"

"How can I trust this man 'Jesus' when I've been abused by so many men?"

"How can I ask my Heavenly Father to put His arms around me and hold me close?"

"How do I know Jesus won't let me down?"

And the question I am most often asked, "How can I entrust my very life to another man?"

I want so badly for you to know that Jesus is not "just another man." Man is born with a carnal nature which, if not under the control of God, is easily given over to crude bodily pleasures and appetites.

Jesus has a divine nature. The word "divine" means *supremely good*! The Jesus I have come to know, to love and to trust is good. He gives good things and only the things that will work for my good.

Yes, He created sex, but never did He intend for it to be abused. He grieves with those of us who have experienced its abuses. I see these precious victims in a continual process of building walls, erecting barriers, distancing themselves from sources of help, burying their hurts and rejecting the arms of a loving Heavenly Father who reaches out to them in compassion.

Fear of the Father

How tragic! What a deceptive work of the enemy! I'll never forget the voice of one very hurting young woman on the telephone.

"Hi. This is Lauren Stratford. How can I help you?" She began to cry. In a broken voice she haltingly got the words out, "I read the first two pages of your book, and I couldn't go any further. I was there with you. It happened to me. I know the smells, the sounds, the pain, the fear."

Her cries turned to sobbing as she finally blurted out the words, "I hate my father! I'll never trust another man!"

"I know, I understand. It's all right," I reassured her. How many times had I heard the same admissions from women who had just read those same two pages? I will never get used to it. I still get a lump in my throat and a sickening feeling in the pit of my stomach as I identify with the tormented anguish of yet another unhealed victim.

As I continued to reassure her that her feelings were perfectly normal, she began to spill out the details of her sexual abuse in descriptions that were nauseating and all too familiar.

I had to work hard at not crying with her.

My feelings of identification were abruptly interrupted when I heard the words, "I'm all alone. No one cares for me. I might as well die!"

Such a disclosure can never be taken lightly, even when made in the distress of the moment. For the better part of an hour, I constantly asked the Lord to speak through me in gently pointing her to Him.

This woman needed an intimate friend to whom she could cry out to anytime, day or night. She needed to feel loved and cared for. She needed healing for a host of deep and gaping wounds. She needed Jesus!

As great as her need was, she resisted the thought of baring her soul to Him. I continued to minister to her, encouraging her to risk her fears in coming to Jesus with her hurts. I ended our conversation by praying with her and telling her that I would call her back in a few days.

Dialing her number again, I wondered how she would sound when she answered. I even feared that perhaps she had carried out her thought of ending her life.

"Hello." The voice was strong and cheery. I thought, "Maybe I dialed the wrong number." (Oh me of little faith!)

"Hi! This is Lauren."

"Oh Lauren, I'm so glad you called! I can't wait to tell you what's happening to me."

For the next twenty minutes, I listened to the testimony of a victim turned into a triumphant survivor because she had risked becoming intimate with Jesus.

"I was lonely, Lauren, but I was afraid to ask Jesus to be a father to me. I wanted to be held and comforted so badly, but I was afraid He'd reject me." She paused for a moment. I heard her swallow hard.

"Lauren, I couldn't go on the way I was any longer. I couldn't stand the hurt. My pain wasn't getting better. It was getting worse. That hurt little girl in me longed to crawl up in Jesus' lap and be rocked back and forth until she didn't hurt anymore."

"What did you do?" I asked. "I know something has happened because you sound so much better."

"Lauren, I was so desperate that I decided I didn't have anything to lose. I got down on my knees and I told Him everything. Everything, Lauren. My hurts, my fears, my anger. I even told Him I had hated Him for not stopping my father from abusing me."

"How did you feel afterward?"

I heard a sigh of relief. As she began to tell me of her experience, her voice reflected the warm glow of God's healing touch. I was right. I heard a story of hurts that were being healed, of aloneness that was replaced with the presence of Jesus, and of hatred that had been turned into love.

I heard a story of a woman who had finally allowed the bitterness of her past to be restored to joy through an intimate encounter with her Heavenly Father.

"You know what, Lauren?" she asked with a voice full of anticipation. "The little girl finally crawled up into Jesus' lap. He put His arms around her and held her so close. For the first time since my father hurt me, I felt loved and secure and protected. I've never felt so close to anyone in my whole life!"

The Miracle of Intimacy

This precious woman's experience is testimony to the miraculous work that happens when people in pain risk intimacy with God. Intimacy forged in the midst of trials. Intimacy that has been born out of a desperate need to be loved by someone who would never reject them. Intimacy that can only be found in Jesus Christ.

Are you hurting so badly that you would just like to end it all? Do your wounds go so deep that they continue to bleed with aching and anguish? Can you echo David's torment of spirit when he mourned, "My spirit is heavy within me. If even one would show some pity, if even one would comfort me!" (Psalm 69:20 TLB).

My friend, Jesus is the one who will comfort you in the deepest hurt of your darkest hour. He will be the father you never had; the love you never received; the warmth you never felt. Because you have known pain, you can know the One who heals pain. Because you have known suffering, you can know the tender touch of the Father's hand. Because you have known aloneness, you can know the intimate Jesus who will be your closest companion.

Have you only heard of a Jesus who is stoic, authoritative and whose chief function is to mete out justice through discipline? Oh, yes, He brings justice, all right. In dying for us, He took our judgment upon Himself. Because of that once-and-for-all sacrifice of love, we who believe are forever perfect in His sight.

And so it is that we are able to look to Him, even though we are only able to utter a faint cry of "Help!" We draw as close as we can. We run to Him with open arms. We find the freedom of laying our head upon His shoulder and soaking His garment with our tears.

Oh, dear one, I invite you to become intimate with God! In the midst of your pain, I invite you to expose the real you—to share, to cry, to express your anger, your sorrow, your bitterness and even your hate.

In return, our loving Lord will grant to you His justice of forgiveness. His mercy. His tenderness. His healing. His restoration to wholeness of life. He will care for you—with love.

– 6 –

"But Lord,
I'm So Weak!"

✦

Only in the past few years have I dared to think and
talk about the terrible parts of my childhood. And I am
more amazed than ever that I withstood them. I am
astounded that I kept my sanity. I was able to keep up
my grades in school. I somehow went to sleep at night.
Most notably, I neither killed myself nor killed my mother.

How could I have been so strong? How could I have
endured such endless abuses without cracking? What
kind of special powers did I have that other children
don't have? Did I have such a deep and unusual love for
my mother that I was willing to take anything she
meted out to me?

The answer is simple—none of the above. I was not
superstrong. I had no powers of my own. And I certainly
did not love my mother. I took her abuses not from
willingness, but because I felt I had no other choice.

After scrubbing the basement steps one day, I stood at
the top of the stairway as she made her usual inspection
of each step—I should say her usual inspection of *every
inch* of every step.

When I saw her run her finger over a certain part of
one of the stairs, then raise her finger up in my face, I
knew three things. First, she had found either dust or
dirt; second, it was on her finger as proof; and third, I
was going to get punished for missing an inch or two in
my scrubbing.

God help me, I actually took a step or two back in anticipation of her anger.

"Don't you back away from me, young lady! You come here and take your punishment, you hear?" she yelled.

How could I help but hear? When my mother was mad, she always yelled loud enough for the entire neighborhood to hear, and I always wondered why no one ever came to find out what was going on.

I took the one or two steps toward her, ready to either get several hard slaps across my face or be spit upon—usually in the vicinity of my eyes. "Normal" punishment didn't seem to be a part of my mother's style. I don't ever remember getting a spanking where most children get spanked!

When I was standing face-to-face with her, maybe only six inches from her, I suddenly felt her foot against my legs. My feet went out from under me and down the stairs I went. Head, feet, arms, legs all rolling and bumping in different directions. It took no more than four or five seconds to stop, and I was about two-thirds of the way down. During those few seconds I heard and felt nothing. But as I lay crumpled in a heap, I realized that my mother was laughing at me, loudly and almost insanely.

"What's the matter? Can't you even keep from tripping over your own feet? Can't you do anything right?" she yelled cruelly.

A sudden and overwhelming surge of hate swelled up within me. I felt like charging up the stairs, picking her up and throwing her down the same stairway. But I was too small, too hurt and too afraid of her.

I also wanted to cry. Tears were always just a flicker away from the barrier of my eyelids. But I had learned all-too-well that I wasn't to cry. My mother couldn't stand for me to cry. I'd like to think it made her feel guilty, but I'm sure there was another reason. I don't know that she ever felt guilty for anything.

I began to move around to see if I had broken any bones, and trying to compose myself. I vaguely heard my mother go outside. The back door opened, then slammed shut. She reappeared at the top of the stairs. As I glanced up, she threw a fistful of dirt at me. It landed everywhere and naturally, as was her intention, most of it landed all over the steps I had just scrubbed.

"Now get up and quit acting like a baby. Clean up this mess. Maybe you can manage to clean these stairs now that you can see where the dirt is," she barked.

Jesus, Be My Strength

I wanted to hide. I wanted to cry. I wanted to scream. I wanted someone to hold me and rock me and comfort me. And most of all, I wanted to run away! But I was only six years old, and too intimidated to do anything other than exactly what my mother ordered.

Another scene was still vivid in my mind, anyway. I had set out from my house just a few months before, wearing only a nightie and slippers, determined to find the police department. I was going to tell them *everything*! A well-intentioned neighbor had seen me outside, picked me up in his arms, and carried me back home.

Now, still crouched on the stairs, I began to shake as I remembered the punishment my mother had given me for trying to run away.[1] I hadn't even begun to recover emotionally from that abuse, and I couldn't think about risking more.

Thank God for the education young children are now given in preschools and early elementary grades about how to say "no," who to go to for help and for the mandatory laws that require school personnel to report suspected child abuse.

After I crawled into bed that night, I waited until my mother was asleep. Then I cried. I sobbed and sobbed until even the mattress was soaked with my tears.

Every muscle ached, and I was bruised all over. But what hurt worst of all was my heart. I wanted my mother to love me, and I knew she didn't.

Alone in my bed with nowhere to turn, with no one else to turn to, I laid my head on my little New Testament and hummed my favorite Sunday School song, "Jesus loves me, this I know . . . little ones to Him belong, we are weak, but He is strong."

Over and over I hummed the melody. Pretty soon it didn't matter so much that I couldn't stand up to my mother or that I was too afraid to run away. As I pictured Jesus sitting on the side of my bed holding me in His arms and wiping the tears from my eyes, even the pain of having no mother's love was lessened.

I was still the same battered little girl. But a man called "Jesus" visited me that night and He was everything I needed. My strength didn't come in a doggedly fierce determination. It didn't come in an ability to tell my mother off. It didn't come in rebelling against her.

My strength came in the gentleness of my Heavenly Father's tender, loving care. My strength came in burying my head in His arms and crying. My strength came in humming a simple little song that told me Jesus loved me and that even though I was weak, it was okay, because He said He would be strong for me.

It was this same Jesus who told me that even though my mother and my father had left me, He would adopt me as His very own special child. I had asked Jesus to be my father and live in my heart at the age of four. The more I look back at such incidents, the more I see how Jesus literally became strength to a little girl who was about as weak as she could be.

Do I Have to Be Strong?

Most of us have been taught that we are to be strong, no matter the circumstance. We are expected to have some great bank of inner resources from which we can draw when trials beat on us like angry warriors. As our earthly father raised us to be strong, we automatically assume that our Heavenly Father demands that same characteristic from us. If we are thinking this way, a downhill plunge is sure to follow at the first sign of weakness. The steps downward are easy to identify. For starters, they begin with a set of faulty assumptions:

"I can't be strong."
"I'm hurting."
"Was I ever strong?"
"I'm getting weaker and weaker."
"God must see me as a failure."
"God doesn't need weak people."
"Therefore, I *am* a failure!"

Maybe you really are a strong person in human terms. But sometimes the "strong" become hurt. Sometimes the "strong" find themselves in a black hole. Sometimes the "strong" find their strength slowly ebbing away. At about that time, the word "weakness" looms larger and larger, circling like a vulture overhead, waiting for the kill. The tragedy is complete when we succumb to that scenario and needlessly allow the vultures to render us disabled.

In talking recently with a woman whose grandchildren had been sexually abused, I heard the voice of a whipped and beaten spirit. This lady is a beautiful Christian. She has lived an exemplary life for Christ, and she loves Him deeply. Yet she was berating herself and feeling so very guilty for "not having what it takes" to rise above the revelations of her grandchildren. She went on to relate a series of events that would make any human being cringe and begin to fold under.

Her voice broke as she admitted, as if she were confessing some horrible sin, "I can't be strong any longer. I'm getting weaker by the day and I feel so guilty. I'm not the Christian I should be."

Feeling guilty? Not the Christian she should be?

I reassured her that she was human, a condition which guarantees weakness, times of emotional drain, and the shedding of tears. "You're reacting the way anyone would under the circumstances. You're living a real-life nightmare."

"Oh Lauren, I needed to hear that! I've felt so guilty because I can't be strong." As her voice sounded relieved, and as she allowed the tears to come, I knew healing was taking place.

"Do you know what you've just done?" I asked her. "You've finally admitted that you are weak; that you can't make it in your own strength. That's what Jesus has been waiting for."

"What do you mean? How can He want me to be weak?" she asked.

"There's a passage of Scripture that I would like to read to you," I answered. I turned in my Bible to 2 Corinthians 12:9 and began to read. "My power shows up best in weak people. Now I am glad to boast about how weak I am; I am glad to be a living demonstration of Christ's power, instead of showing off my own power and abilities" (TLB).

"Who had more trials than the apostle Paul?" I asked her. Listen to them.

- ✦ Prison numerous times.
- ✦ Whipped more times than he could remember.
- ✦ Faced death over and over again.
- ✦ Beaten with 39 lashes five times and with rods three times.
- ✦ Stoned once.
- ✦ Shipwrecked three times.
- ✦ In danger from flooded rivers.

✦ Almost mobbed to death.
✦ Forced to spend sleepless nights.
✦ Went without food.
✦ Endured cold without sufficient clothing.

After reading her the list of Paul's trials I asked, "Do you know what Paul's response was to his nightmare?"

"I can't remember offhand, but I know what my response would be. I'd be so beaten down I'd be dragging!"

"Believe me," I agreed, "I would be too! And that's exactly what Paul said, with no apology or guilt. Paul said that he would only boast about the things that showed how weak he was for then when people saw that he was nothing but a mass of weakness, they would see Jesus become his strength."

A weak Paul became a strong Paul because of Jesus Christ!

Paul is saying, "It's okay to be weak, for in your weakness you enable Christ to reveal His strength!" We are created in weakness and frailty. Our very life, our every breath is dependent upon Christ. Our very humanness makes us weak.

Do I have the power to make my heart beat? Am I the one who empowers my life's blood to flow through my veins? Do I have the power to add one day to my life?

"New Age" thought may say that the power is within me, and I have all that is necessary to create my own reality and destiny. I assure you that lie emanates from the master deceiver, Satan. If I believe that line of reasoning, then when I am hurting and I can't seem to pull myself up by the bootstraps, it's my fault. And if it's my fault, of course it creates one mighty big chunk of guilt!

Marie Chapian, author and therapist, writes, "Your natural weakness is your pathway to spiritual strength. From this moment on refer to weakness not as an enemy, for weakness opens the way to [Christ's] power."[2]

Hurting one, don't look upon your weakness as a feared enemy. Rather see it as your invitation to receive God's strength. Let your weakness work for you, not against you.

When I said this to the grandmother, she wasn't too sure about it. "But Lauren," she asked inquisitively, "my faith is so weak, how in the world could it work *for* me? We're talking about the weakest of the weak here!"

Just how *little* is *weak* faith and how *much* is *strong* faith? Where does one draw the line? Is there some measure by which our faith is good enough or big enough or strong enough that it's sufficient to get the job done? And is there another measure by which our faith is so bad or so little or so weak that we might as well quit and give up?

"How big is a grain of sand?" I replied to her. "How big is a mustard seed? Not very! Yet Jesus says that faith as small as a grain of mustard seed is sufficient to move a mountain! In our sight that's too small to get any job done. But with God's touch upon that tiny seed, it's more than enough!"

The truth of the matter is, the only time our weakness becomes a detriment to us is when we choose to live in our own strength. When we refuse to trust our weakness to the Father, He cannot perfect His strength in us. Do you realize that you cannot be weak in Christ? You can only be weak in yourself.

What the world sees as weakness, Jesus sees as opportunity!

My weakness in my anger and hatred and hurt at my mother pushing me down the stairs was an opportunity for Jesus to rush to my aid and comfort me. It was okay for me to fall into Jesus' arms. It was okay for my weakness to summon the aid of my Heavenly Father. It was okay that I could not be strong in myself. I wasn't looking for a chance for Jesus to love me in a moment of crisis, but when the crisis came, He was there. And that's what mattered!

Weakness Is Frightening

It's a terrifying experience to feel weak. It's frightening to feel as if you can't go one more day, one more mile, through one more hurt. It's devastating to sense that you're teetering on the edge of a cliff, and if just one more thing comes your way you'll go over. You've said to yourself, "I'll never make it. I'll go crazy." It's almost as if we're telling God, "Lord, if You send one more trial I'll die."

No, you're not alone! I've said it, too.

Several years ago, when I was at one of my lowest points, I told God, "I can't make it through whatever else You have planned for me. (At that time in my life I thought He was staying up nights thinking what test He could put me through next!)

The next morning I was reading The Radio Bible Class' daily devotional, "Our Daily Bread." The thought for the day was titled, "Live By The Day!" The Scripture was: "... as thy days, so shall thy strength be" (Deuteronomy 33:25 KJV).

God, I thought to myself, *are You trying to tell me something?* I was almost tempted to not read on. I really hated it when I was feeling bad and God gave me a reason to cheer up! Fortunately, I continued to read, and am I ever thankful! The second paragraph quoted the famous evangelist, Dwight L. Moody. He said:

> A man can no more take in a supply of grace for the future than he can eat enough today to last him for the next 6 months. Nor can he inhale sufficient air into his lungs with one breath to sustain life for a week to come. We are permitted to draw upon God's store of grace from day to day *as we need it*![3]

Well, I began to think about it! And the more I thought about it, the more I realized that this man was right on! I don't need strength for tomorrow—not today, anyway. What's more, I don't need to be reassured that nothing unpleasant will happen tomorrow. When tomorrow comes, my Father will provide whatever I need to make it through—at the proper time!

At first, I was encouraged. But dare I become too peaceful, or God forbid, actually triumphant, Satan sneaked in a "but what" doubt. Here it came.

"But what about today, Lord? I don't feel like I can make it through until this afternoon, much less tomorrow."

The "but whats," "what abouts," "what ifs," "yeah, buts," were always there to put a damper on any encouragement that came from the Lord.

As I was busy stretching out "today" as if it were an eternity, three words jumped out from the page— "moment to moment." *Moment to moment! I thought. I can do that! I can make it for that long!* And with that truth under my belt, Satan's doubts weren't nearly as threatening.

We don't need strength for tomorrow any more than we need breath for tomorrow. It is in my *present* weakness—the "now"—when I need Jesus. It's for the weakness of this very moment that I need His strength and power.

When I was at the bottom of the stairs after my mother had pushed my feet out from under me, I wasn't worrying if Jesus would be around tomorrow. I needed Him right then. It was my very position of weakness that summoned Him to be my strength. It was that very immediate cry, "Help, Lord," that unleashed His strength.

Moody was right. The Lord never gives us His strength in advance. Our Lord makes the same statement when He says, "Do not worry about tomorrow, for tomorrow will worry about itself. Each day has enough trouble of its own." My weakness will be His strength today—for *this* hour; for *this* moment; for *this* trial.

Are They Superhumans?

Where did the early Christians get the courage to face the Roman Coliseum, well aware that starved lions would soon come roaring out of their cages to devour them?

Where did they get the courage to march resolutely to the stake, knowing that piles of kindling would soon blaze with fire all around them?

What gives servants of Jesus Christ in Communist countries the courage to pass out Christian tracts on street corners knowing they will be sentenced to years in prison for doing so? Or to secretly gather deep in the forests to worship and pray, risking detection by the KGB and almost certain sentencing?

Are such people superhuman? Do they have no fear? Have they no frailties? Can you believe that they are made of the same dust as you and me? Ah, but they are mere mortals, into whom God has breathed the breath of life. Their frame is just like ours.

If so, then what is their secret?

There is no secret! Whose heart would not beat a little faster and harder when standing in the path of a lion racing toward him! Who would not wish himself anywhere but tied to a stake, when the flames began to lick at his feet!

So how did they make it through? Here is the answer. A simple trust in the God of their salvation promised them that He would be their strength in their moment of tribulation.

I can't imagine that they were making jokes in their holding cells before being marched into the coliseum arena, boasting to each other, "Man, this is nothing. I'll whip those lions bare-handed!"

Rather, I can see them kneeling in prayer, hand in hand, asking God to be their strength and shield in time of trouble. I can hear some of the women quietly weeping. I can see them giving each other tearful kisses of brotherly love and bidding farewell until meeting again on the other shore.

It is almost too painful for me to even think about their sufferings. Those precious saints were not equal to the battle. The weakness of their human frames was not equal to the evilness of the Roman rulers' schemes. Their courage was not theirs, but the Lord's! Their strength was not theirs. It was the Lord's!

And so I say to you who hurt, who are weak, who are fearful, who are weary and discouraged—

> The battle is not yours.
> It is the Lord's!
> Stand still.
> Tell Him your fears.
> Listen for His voice.
> Hear Him speak peace to you.
> Receive His strength.
> Whatever the burden,
> God will proportion His strength
>   for you to bear up under it.

His strength is greater than your weakness!

– 7 –

Oh, the Masks We Wear!

◆

Can you really know me? Do I really see you? Or are we hiding behind masks, disguising our real selves? Why do we wear them? From what or whom are we hiding? What do we fear?

Some of us have become so accustomed to wearing our masks that they have become an inseparable part of us. We have played our game of hiding for so long and so well that reality has all but disappeared.

Why is it that we are hidden behind masks?

Are we too proud?
Are we afraid we'll be pitied?
Are we ashamed?
Do we feel guilty?
Are we afraid our hurt will be minimized or misunderstood?
Are we afraid we'll get a sermon on "shaping up"?
Have we been taught it's "unChristian" to show our hurt?
Do we want to be left alone in our hurt?

I'm Going Crazy!

Each of us who hides behind a mask may have a different reason for doing so, but we all share the same diagnosis—hurt. And for one or many of the above reasons, we have chosen to hide that hurt behind a mask—a mask we tie tighter and tighter around ourselves as old hurts deepen and new hurts are added. We take our masks off for no one, not for our spouse, not for our closest friend, not for our pastor, not even for Jesus!

One Sunday my pastor preached about allowing ourselves to be ourselves. The illustration he used stands out vividly in my mind.

"When you come into the morning service and your friend approaches you eagerly with the typical greeting, 'Hi Doris, how are you?' and you answer with the typical, 'Just fine, Sherry,' I want to know: Are you telling the truth?

"Or," he continued, "are you really thinking behind that forced smile, 'I'm feeling horrible, Sherry! Gary and I got into an argument on the way to church. He wants to go right home after the service to watch his stupid football game on TV, and I want to go out to eat.

" 'Meanwhile, the kids were in the backseat, turning the car into a combat zone. Peter was yelling, "I want to go home! Stop the car! Let me out!" He doesn't like Sunday School at the moment. Tracy was crying at the top of her lungs, because she wanted to wear the new dress I got her for Easter and I didn't let her.' "

My pastor ended the illustration by saying, "Doris really wanted to shout to everyone walking through the front doors, "I can't stand my family! My husband's nothing but a self-centered jerk! My kids are driving me up the wall! AND I'M GOING CRAZY!"

Everyone in the congregation laughed, understanding perfectly. It's true. We are raised and taught to act in the manner that is expected of us. If we are feeling otherwise, then we had best pretend.

And on goes the mask!

Who Are You—Really?

I was speaking at a women's retreat last year that was held at a campground in the mountains. Part of my talk was on the subject of wearing masks. I looked at the women seated around me in a semicircle and asked, "Who is the real you behind the mask you're wearing? When you drove up the mountains yesterday, who was the real person sitting behind the steering wheel?"

I began to slowly scan each face. There was dead silence. "Am I seeing the real you as I look into your eyes, or am I seeing the mask you've been wearing for a week, a month, or perhaps even for years?"

Several women lowered their heads. After talking with so many women who are hurting, the Lord has helped me to look behind their "disguises." I said nothing for a few moments sensing a mountain of deep hurts that were begging for attention. I silently prayed, "Oh God, help me to say something that will minister to these dear women. Help them to take their masks off, and heal their wounds."

At breakfast the next morning my eyes were barely open. The crisp mountain air did nothing to revive my weary body. I looked across the breakfast table and saw women whose smiles beat mine by a mile! I was beginning to feel just a little out of place with my half-open eyes and cheerless expression.

"Did I miss something or what?" I quickly asked myself.

I ate my breakfast in relative silence. I wasn't up to the wide-awake conversation my participation would have demanded. The breakfast menu was so unimpressive I don't remember one thing I ate. What followed, however, was anything but dull.

One by one, during the course of the day, women began to confide in me. Their stories were identical down to the commas and periods. So were the looks on their faces—the same looks I had seen across the breakfast table. It took a couple of stories for me to catch on, but after that I didn't have to ask any questions. I knew what they were going to say.

The first sentence was, "I was one of the women you were talking about yesterday when you asked how many of us were wearing masks to hide our hurts."

I would nod my head as each would continue. "I've worn my mask for years and I've never taken it off . . . until last night in our small-group sharing time. I finally took it off and shared my hurts for the first time."

"How did you feel about it?" I would ask. The answer was obvious, but I wanted to hear it anyway. "Oh Lauren, I felt so free! I was free to be myself. I was free to show the real me with all my hurts and my fears. I even cried."

I was also pretty sure of the answer to my next question. "How did the other women react to the real you?"

"You know, Lauren. They put their arms around me and cried with me. I felt so loved. I never dreamed anyone would love me for the real me with my doubts and feelings of guilt and worthlessness. But they did!"

As was the same with each woman, the looks on their faces could best be described as "relief" and "joy"—*real* joy.

How full my heart was as they shared with me, for I knew firsthand how healing it is for a mask to come off. I was listening to a cassette tape of that talk the other day. I heard my voice begin to break as I admitted, "If I had only been willing to take my mask off twenty years ago, who knows what horrors I might have been spared?"

"Do me a favor," I told those women. "Don't ever put your mask back on. In fact, just throw it away. You don't need it anymore!"

Which Mask Do You Wear?

I suppose the mask we are the most familiar with is

the "I'm fine" mask. You know—the smile (though somewhat forced), the sparkling eyes (though sometimes dulled), the rosy cheeks (thank goodness for makeup), and so on. All of us have put on that mask from time to time. And most of us wear it well. But there are other masks we wear, perhaps not so obvious, but nonetheless serving the same function of covering up real feelings.

The "Expressionless Face" mask: I'm really good at this one. I've heard so many comments like, "I wish I could be like you. You take everything in stride. You never get upset or angry or frustrated. How can you always be in such control?"

Meanwhile I'm thinking to myself, "If you only knew what I'm feeling on the inside!"

The reality is that I sometimes cover my true feelings with a mask of indifference, nonchalance and an undisturbed calmness. My expressionless face says "Nothing affects me. I never get bent out of shape or out of sorts with anything." This belies the truth. I'm really holding back a mighty rushing wall of emotions that I'm afraid to let my face register.

The "Keeping Myself Busy" mask: Many of us grab for this one. It's readily available and easy to put on. Busy at home. Busy at church. Busy on the job. Busy at fun.

The truth is, being busy is often a way of running away from our hurts. The busier we are, the less time we have to think about them. That may be true, but oftentimes, the kindest thing we can do for ourselves is to stop wearing the "busyness" mask, to slow down or even take a complete break. In this way we will be able to give undivided attention to the healing of our hurts.

The "Keeping Out of View" mask: When in pain, some of us go into seclusion. We hide not only from ourselves, but from everyone else, too. The public becomes our "enemy" when we feel our mask isn't adequate. Behind the privacy of our own doors we "lick our wounds." And only when our inward barometer of feelings says "fair weather" do we let ourselves be seen.

Unfortunately, keeping to ourselves usually ends up being harmful. The longer we're alone, the worse we feel. Our personal agonies loom larger as we cut ourselves off from communicating with others.

The "I'm All Dressed Up" mask: Anyone who is all dressed up just has to be feeling fine. Right? The assumption is that looking good on the outside means feeling good on the inside.

Of course "looking good" can be nothing more than a mask we're wearing—our attempt to disguise "feeling bad." A fancy dress or a business suit and designer tie doesn't always reflect the feelings of the heart. You may be the epitome of fashion, yet feel as though your heart were wrapped in rags.

In addition to these, there are masks you wear that I don't, and vice versa. But they all serve the same function. They hide hurts that need healing. We need to identify our masks, and we need to understand why we are wearing them. Even if they have benefited us for a season, they may now be hindering us from receiving our healing.

Can I See the Real You?

I ask each of you, "Who is the real you?" If you were to look at yourself in the mirror, and if you were to be honest with yourself, would you be looking at the *real* you (and only you know who that is), or would you be looking at a mask?

Once we are able to admit we are wearing a mask, we have taken a step toward healing. Some of us have worn our masks for so long, have pretended to be something else for so long, that we don't even know what is behind the disguise. We have managed to fool ourselves along with everyone else!

It takes a deep work of the Holy Spirit to sort out all of the hurts we have kept in protective custody and the reasons we have put them there. Some of us have buried our hurts so deeply within our subconscious that only the Lord Himself can resurface them. But one thing is certain, no matter how deeply they are buried and seemingly forgotten, they are still there—*unhealed* and *destructive*.

Or maybe your hurts are always just beneath the surface threatening to expose themselves at the most inopportune moment. You may be well aware of them, constantly on guard lest your mask fails and your hurts are exposed.

There is not a person who hasn't been hurt and felt it necessary to hide that hurt away. We bury our hurts for one or both of the following reasons:

1. We don't want to deal with them.

2. We don't know how to handle them.

Whichever the reason, or if it is for both reasons, we know only one way to address the unsolved problem. We put on a mask, which does two things:

1. It hides our true feelings.

2. It gives a false appearance.

I've received letters from persons who have written comments such as, "I live with a family who loves me, but they don't know me!" How tragic to be one person on the outside and a completely different person on the inside. Yet this circumstance invariably arises when we fear that our hurts or sins will prevent us from being accepted the way we really are.

A number of women have sent me photos of themselves with their letters. Some look so beautiful, so alive, so "all-American!" And yet, on the back of the photo are words like, "You might think I'm pretty, but I'm not. This isn't the real me!"

One woman wrote, "You've got a photo that tells you an outside story, but the inside story is ugly and scary."

How I long to meet personally with each woman. How I would like to sit with her and talk about her hurts.

What Would I Tell You?

If you were one of those women, I would tell you that hidden, unattended hurts don't go away. They don't even stay the same. They grow bigger and deeper. And they never heal! Hidden hurts grow from *hurt* to *Hurt* to *HURT*! The pain gets worse. The resentment grows. If there is guilt, it begins to gnaw away.

I would tell you that your mask has become a Band-Aid, covering up the injury, but bringing about no healing. Band-Aids trap our hurts behind a protective covering rather than allowing the light of exposure to start the healing process.

Wounds need light. Initially, perhaps, a Band-Aid provides a buffer zone, a neutral area that temporarily protects or separates us from the conflict.

That's fine. We often need to step back from the initial wounding. We are in a period of shock or trauma, and it is just too painful to roll up our sleeves and say, "Let's get on with the healing process."

But the danger is, having retreated, we are tempted to remain in that neutral area.

No one wants to confront pain, to bring it out in the open. So instead of our distancing period being only temporary, it becomes permanent. And our wounds stay in the dark behind the bandaging of the mask we've put on.

When little Tommy pleads with his mother, "Please Mommy, don't pull the Band-Aid off. It'll hurt!" Does Mommy say, "All right, honey, Mommy won't pull it off because she doesn't want you to hurt"?

I hope Mommy doesn't say that! I hope she says, "Tommy, I know it's going to hurt, but the Band-Aid has to come off so the air can get to your 'owie.' The air will make it get all better. I know it will hurt to pull the Band-Aid off, but it will only hurt for a moment."

Our Band-Aid masks must come off. We cannot afford to hide behind them forever. Why? Because our wounds desperately need to be exposed to the healing touch of the Lord Jesus.

"But Lauren, I'm so afraid to take my mask off. People will see the real me, and they won't like what they see."

Do you remember the women at the mountain retreat I talked about earlier who told me they had dared to take their masks off for the first time? Without exception, each one shared an experience of being loved and cared for and accepted. Not one said, "They looked horrified," or "They acted like they were disgusted," or "I think they were disappointed in the real me."

When I took my mask off, when I quit working so hard to hide my wounds of abuse and hurt, do you know that my friends liked me better! That is the honest truth! People told me, "I thought you were stuck up, because you always stood off from the rest of us." Others said, "I thought you were the only one of us who didn't hurt because you never shared any hurts with us.

"Now I know you're for real, and I like you so much better."

Never in my wildest imagination did I dream that I had done such a good job of hiding behind my mask! To learn that there were actually people who thought I had never gone through any hurt—that was inconceivable!

It was almost as hard to realize that my friends were more caring and more loving toward me after I unwrapped all of the bandages that I had worn for so long and showed my hurts to them. Yet it was true. I couldn't deny the change in them and in me.

How did that change happen? When did it happen? Did it happen overnight? Was it easy, or was it hard?

There are few parts of this book I will enjoy writing as much as this one. For what I'm about to share with you has been one of the most transforming events in my life.

For several years, I had dared to share some of the painful parts of my past. Little by little, slowly but surely, I would risk telling someone one or two things. But I would only tell those things that I had carefully weighed beforehand and determined them to be the least risky.

The usual response was, "I'm sorry, and I'll be praying for you." And that was that. There wasn't much more they could do. Occasionally, rejection came, and one particular rejection caused me to close up again for more than a year.

After spending fifteen or twenty minutes at the altar praying and crying at a church I attended, I noticed the pastor's wife standing a few feet away. I felt so alone and I wanted to just be loved for a few seconds. I walked over to her and put my arms around her to give her a hug. That was a big step for me. I seldom risked that kind of closeness.

I sensed that she was feeling a little awkward about it so I quickly withdrew my arms. She said something kind to me. I knew she cared, but wasn't the hugging type.

What happened the next morning was the problem—a major problem!

My phone rang. I answered, and heard my pastor's voice. "My wife told me that you really held on to her last night at church. You know, Lauren, we can't be a family to you, if that's what you're wanting. You must realize that."

I was stunned. Speechless. Devastated. "Where did he get the idea I wanted them to be a family to me?" The question raced through my mind. All I had wanted was a hug!

I was so taken back that I hung up on him. I think that's the only time I have ever hung up on anyone.

Taking off our masks is a risk. Occasionally we will be bruised by someone's insensitivity. And yet the ultimate benefits certainly outweigh the dangers. One of the greatest blessings we receive is that, by sharing our needs with others, they begin to pray for us. And I cannot overstate the importance of the one single act of prayer.

I had no one, for years upon years. I shared with no one. I never felt arms of love around me. I truly felt at times like I was wandering alone in the middle of a vast desert. But I know beyond a shadow of a doubt that God always had someone praying for me.

When I got to the point where I was at "rock bottom," Jesus performed a miracle that even I could not have dared to hope for. I share it with you as a hope for your life that Jesus never intended for His children to walk through this life alone. And though He may not answer the cry of your heart in the same manner that He chose to answer mine, He will answer it in the way that is best for you.

I know. He did it for me.

Morning Dawns!

Beyond my tears was a future brightly colored with hope, joy, laughter, fulfillment, love, many hugs—I could go on forever naming the beautiful flowers in my garden!

For so long I had viewed life through a veil of tears. Something better was beyond, but those tears of hurt and crises were always there to cloud my vision, and I just couldn't see what was beyond them. Words like "joy," "hope" and "beauty" were but blurred images in the distance. They were there, but they were not attainable.

Morning dawned for me with a voice on the other end of a phone line. "Yes, I'll meet with you and I'll listen to you," Johanna Michaelsen said. At that moment, a little light streamed through my tears. But wouldn't you know that just when Jesus was providing me a hope for the future, I began to doubt it?

"Am I doing the right thing?"

"I don't even know her."

"What if she changes her mind?"

"What if she doesn't like me?"

I had read about Johanna's unique background in her book *The Beautiful Side of Evil.* I had seen her on television. I had been tremendously impressed with her and was fully aware that she would understand my past experiences and the horrors that continued to haunt me. But how close I came to not keeping that appointment! Looking back, it makes me shudder to think what my life might still be like if I had listened to my own doubts and fears.

I guess that is why I am so quick to encourage others to risk taking that first step when God begins to do something new in their lives. *New* is risky. *Change* is fearsome. But when God is in it, when He is the author of it, we simply must take those first unsteady steps. Praise God, I somehow took them in spite of my fears!

And yes, I was doing the right thing. Johanna didn't change her mind. She and her husband did like me. Most importantly, they accepted me unconditionally. I only asked that they listen to me and give me some advice. In addition, they gave me love, understanding and support. Eventually, they became a brother and a sister to me.

I thank Johanna and Randolph for what they have given to me and for what they have become to me, but I give the glory and praise to Jesus, for He is the One who worked through them to perform the miracle.

It was a risk to tell Johanna many of my secrets. Talk about taking a mask off. I wasn't even sure my mask *would* come off! I had worn it for so long it was molded to my face. But when God is in the process, things just seem to happen without our having to work at them. By the time I walked out of their office, that old mask had just sort of melted off my face and disappeared without my even realizing it. When God does the work, everything fits together. And it's beautiful!

Up until that time, I had seen God do some glorious things, *but not for me.* I am sure some of you feel the same way. You watch blessings come into the lives of your friends and other family members. In the meantime it seems as though nothing but trials and tribulations beat a path to your door.

That's one reason you are wearing a mask.

Let me explain two things. First, I walked through life *without* a Johanna for many, many years. Sometimes He chooses to work through people at specific times. But during those earlier years, I found Jesus to be my everything. I would not then, nor would I now trade Jesus and His love for anyone or anything else. My life must always depend on Him first, not on any person or experience.

I would also like to encourage you with my belief that Jesus will be faithful to bring to you exactly what or who you need—at exactly the right moment. If I didn't believe that, I might as well not even bother to finish this book, for it would be a book without hope. In fact, I might as well throw my Bible away. Because Jesus says that He will supply everything we need.

Perhaps the key to your door won't be turned by a Johanna. It may happen in a way you never dreamed possible. We can never imagine what or when or how the Lord Jesus is going to meet our needs. But one thing is certain—*He will!*

Taking the Risk

There's an old saying. I don't know where it came from and I probably can't quote it word for word, but it goes something like this: "The ship is safe in the harbor. But it will never reach its destination if it doesn't leave the harbor."

You and I will never reach our destination if we don't take some necessary chances. My need had to reach beyond my fear when I drove to my first meeting with Johanna. When the Lord Jesus opens a door for you, your need will never be met if you don't leave the safety of the barriers you have erected.

In the lives of others, I've seen the Lord open doors only to have the person too afraid to risk walking through them.

It was a major disappointment when my attempt to reach out to my pastor's wife was rejected. After that, I must admit I didn't attend church for a year-and-a-half. Eventually I just got too starved spiritually to stay away any longer. I couldn't continue not worshiping with a congregation. On the other hand, I didn't want to be hurt again!

I had visited a certain church once before. I liked it, but was unwilling to risk being the real me in it, and I was determined I would never call another church my home where I couldn't be myself.

And so I made a "game plan." I decided that I would make an office appointment with the pastor and lay all my cards out on the table, so to speak. I would say, "This is who I am. This is where I've come from. This is my past. This is what I'm doing now. Will you accept me *just the way I am*? If you won't, that's okay. Just tell me up front and I won't start attending your church."

I did just what I planned to do. I sat in the pastor's office, told him my story, then watched the expression on his face as I waited for his answer.

This guy blew me away! He looked about as unruffled as anyone I have ever seen. His voice was calm. You would have thought he had heard the same story ten times already that day. "What am I supposed to say?" he inquired, almost as if he didn't understand what the big deal was about. "Of course you can come. You're more than welcome!"

I sat there for a moment, giving him a chance to change his mind. Nothing more came out of his mouth. I got up and muttered something like, "Thank you," and I turned to leave.

"See you Sunday," he called to me.

For over a year, I attended that church in anonymity. I was writing *Satan's Underground* and I had asked the pastor (during our famous meeting) to keep everything I had shared with him confidential. He did. I sat in the back row and was usually the first one to leave every Sunday.

Then the real test came. My book was completed and would be in the bookstores within the month. I phoned my pastor and told him that *Satan's Underground* was about to come out and that I thought it was time to tell the congregation. He agreed.

I cannot tell you the fear in my heart as I walked into the sanctuary the following Sunday morning. I sat down and looked around. "I wonder if any of these people will ever speak to me again?"

Thank God my pastor penciled in the part about me near the beginning of the service. At least it would soon be over! He called me to the pulpit and began to talk about my writing *Satan's Underground* and what the book was about. I was too scared to look at the faces in the congregation. But I surely caught my pastor's last remarks.

"Folks, let me tell you the way I feel about Lauren. If you don't like her being here or you can't accept her past, then you can leave. Because she's staying!"

"Oh dear Jesus, what has he done? Half the church will get up and leave!" During the remainder of the service my mind stayed busy planning how I would get out of the sanctuary without anyone seeing me. Once I heard the "Amen" at the end of the service, I jumped up to hurry toward the side door. But I couldn't get into the aisle.

People were coming toward me from every direction. Some with smiles. Some with tears. But all with a look of love! Arms reached out to hug me or pat me gently on my back. I'm not sure how I reacted because I was so overwhelmed.

I should know by now that that's the way Jesus does things—*in His time. Perfectly. Beautifully. Warmly. With so much love!*

Was I taking a risk when I took off my mask in the pastor's office three years ago? I thought I was. Could he have turned me away? I thought he could. Was I taking a risk when I allowed him to tell the whole church what he had been keeping in confidence for over a year? I thought I was. Could the congregation have rejected me? I thought so.

But it didn't happen that way.

I have been worshiping there since *Satan's Underground* came out. My church carries the book in their bookstore and many in the congregation have read it. If anything, I feel more loved and supported.

I urge you to risk that vulnerable feeling of being transparent. The enemy wants us to think that in opening ourselves to transparency we are liable to receive punishment or rejection. If Satan is whispering that in your ear, you can be sure that the very opposite is true! When you take that kind of risk, you rob Satan of the joy he finds in keeping you miserable. Better yet, you give Jesus the opportunity to heal you. Giving the enemy a black eye and receiving healing at the same time is a deal you can't afford to pass up!

The Danger of Self-Pity

The differences in our hurts do not lie in degree, in intensity, or in duration. Pain is pain. The differences in our hurts are revealed by how each of us chooses to deal with them.

Will your hurt rule you and keep you a prisoner hidden behind the barriers you have erected? Or will you choose to break down those barriers and allow Jesus to lovingly bind up your hurts in His love?

When we allow ourselves to yield to the desire of excessively dwelling on our problems without choosing God's positive alternatives, we are giving in to self-pity. We are giving free rein to the harmful emotion of feeling sorry for ourselves.

It is a little like falling into a deep hole. Once we have fallen into self-pity, it's hard to climb out. We tend to sink deeper and deeper until we are drowning. We find ourselves totally incapable of receiving solutions and healing. In fact, we reach a point where we really don't want answers. We have wrapped our personal identity up in our problems, and we have learned to enjoy our pain, in a perverse sort of way.

Our masks often hide the results of the pity parties we have indulged in. I speak from firsthand experience. I once nearly succumbed to my hurts, never allowing anyone else to see them, but secretly entertaining them behind my mask. Today, however, at last my hurts are being healed. I have no reason to feel sorry for myself any longer! By the grace of God, my journey to wholeness has left self-pity far behind.

But maybe that sounds easier said than done. How do we turn our negative perceptions around?

We think:

◆ I was abused sexually...therefore, I am dirty and no good.

- ✦ My husband left me...therefore, I am un-
  lovable.

- ✦ I sinned...therefore, I am unforgivable.

- ✦ My son is on drugs...therefore, I have failed
  as a parent.

- ✦ My husband had an affair...therefore, I
  am a bad wife.

- ✦ I'm overweight...therefore, I am ugly.

- ✦ I don't make much money...therefore, I am
  a poor provider.

- ✦ I think immoral thoughts...therefore, I am
  evil.

- ✦ I'm easily depressed...therefore, I must be
  mentally ill.

- ✦ I didn't do well in school...therefore, I am
  dumb.

- ✦ It's hard for me to trust God...therefore,
  I'm not a good Christian.

The list could be endless. I'm sure you could name some perceptions of yourself that I've missed. There are hundreds of negatives that we could attach to ourselves. And the enemy of our souls would just love for us to claim every one!

Changing our perspective sounds like it must be a near impossibility but it isn't. The trick is to turn our eyes in another direction. We have to stop looking at ourselves and our outward situations. We need to start looking to Jesus and the heart within us, our inner self.

Jesus says, "And be not conformed to this word: but be ye transformed by the renewing of your mind..." (Romans 12:2 KJV).

We can try to change every situation we don't like. We can try to forget every experience that has hurt us. We can change our physical appearance. But if we still have negative perceptions of ourselves, or thoughts of self-pity, we're still in trouble.

Jesus, the wonderful counselor, can do a work of healing on our inner man, our mind, our heart, our spirit. His love is able to teach us a right way of thinking about ourselves.

Jesus... transforming the young woman who was a sexually abused child by a cleansing and healing of her mind and heart.

Jesus... transforming the precious one who fights depression with a renewing of the mind.

Jesus... transforming the Christian who struggles with trusting God by a healing of the heart.

I condemn myself. I am my own judge and jury. But as a Christian, I am wrong. Romans 8:1 says, "There is therefore now no condemnation to them which are in Christ Jesus..." (KJV). We may condemn ourselves, but Jesus pronounces us "Not Guilty!" Others may accuse us, but Jesus throws out the accusations. *No condemnation* is one of the greatest privileges of the Christian. All too many of us, however, fail to take advantage of this privilege. We continue to live in the same condemnation and guilt we lived in when we were without Christ.

Yet, regardless of the experiences we have had, regardless of the situations we are in right now, regardless of what anyone else tells us, we have some gifts from Jesus which are our inheritance.

Forgiveness	Healing
Cleansing	Wholeness
Purity	A Sound Mind

We can choose to think on things that are:

True	Honest
Just	Pure
Lovely	Of good report

We can choose to see ourselves as Jesus sees us.

A new creature!	Transformed!
Whole!	Unique!
Special!	Chosen!
His son!	His daughter!

It is my privilege and my right, and I might even say my obligation, to see myself exactly the way my Heavenly Father sees me. He created me. He examines me. He knows me. He is my judge. Now if He has pronounced me forgiven and new and whole and clean and transformed, then that's exactly what I am.

The scars we bear from a wounded body and heart only say that we have been through a battle and have emerged as survivors. Our scars do not change who we are! We may bear them proudly as we stand alongside our Savior who also bears scars from a deep wounding.

Jesus is a survivor! And so are you! Don't allow your scars to keep portraying you as a victim.

I was a victim for years. Now Jesus has delivered me from my position as a victim, and I refuse to continue to see myself as one. In so many interviews for the media (television and radio) this past year, I have been asked to participate as "the victim." One of these days I am going to stand up in the middle of a live TV show and put my hands up to my mouth and yell, "I'm not a victim anymore!

"I am forgiven! I am cleansed! I am healed and made whole! I am delivered from my prison! I am free! I am a child of my Heavenly Father!"

And you, too, are a child of your Heavenly Father. He will never see you as anything else or anything less! You will always be His child! If you have problems seeing yourself as your Father sees you (and that's who you really are!), please memorize the following Scripture.

Remind yourself of it as often as you need to be reassured.

> And so we should not be like cringing, fearful slaves, but we should behave like God's very own children, adopted into the bosom of his family, and calling to him, "Father, Father." For his Holy Spirit speaks to us deep in our hearts, and tells us that we really are God's children (Romans 8:15,16 TLB).

That is a great truth. We are God's children, adopted into the bosom of His family!

If Jesus loved us enough to give His life for us, He must love us very, very much! Should we not view ourselves through His eyes? If we were worth enough to cost the life of Jesus Christ, then we're worth enough to be our real selves. I'm going to choose to act like the child of God that I am.

Will you make the same choice with me?

Taking Your Rightful Place

I was listening to Lee Ezell, the beautiful author of *The Cinderella Syndrome* and *The Missing Piece*, on a Christian television program. Using the Bird of Paradise flower as an illustration, she presented a beautiful message about being "the real you." I hastily found a pencil and wrote down some words that brightened my day with bold and vivid colors:

> Being the real you does not change your place in the kingdom of Jesus Christ, nor does it cancel your validity as a Child of God.

Holding up a Bird of Paradise, Lee went on to explain. True, that peculiar-looking flower was different, all right! It certainly was unique. But its uniqueness did not change its place in the flower kingdom. No matter what it looked like or what others thought of it, it was still a flower, and it would never be anything else.

I, for one, don't particularly care for the Bird of Paradise. But my opinion will never change its looks. It will continue to grow just the way God created it. If it gets buffeted by the winds or pelted by the rains or trampled on by a child chasing a ball, it will still display its true colors.

I say to you the same thing. Nothing, *absolutely nothing that happens to you* will change your value in the kingdom of Jesus Christ. Winds may buffet, rains may pelt you. Someone along the way, perhaps even a friend, may step on you and crush you into the ground. You will be tempted to hide. Don't run! Don't hide! Don't put on a mask!

From my heart to your heart, I encourage you to find out who the real Jesus is. In finding Him, you will find yourself. From Him, you will receive the courage you need *to be you*.

– 8 –

The Garden of My Tears

✦

Tears.

There is probably no subject I know more about. And there is no chapter I have dreaded writing more than this one. Yesterday, I sat at my desk and stared at a blank piece of paper most of the day. When I woke up this morning, I could still see that empty piece of paper lying on the desk. I knew it was there, not a word on it.

After making coffee, which usually is a warm, cozy time for me, I dragged myself up the stairs. Coffee cup in hand, I said firmly, "I'm going to walk into that study, sit down at my desk and write this chapter on tears. And I am not going to cry!"

It is now thirty minutes later. My coffee cup is empty. My eyes are full of tears. And soon they will be making their all-too-familiar pathway down my face.

Fortunately, the Lord began to speak to my heart. "All right, Lord," I responded. "I'll listen, but I think I already know what You're going to say, and it's going to make me cry."

In His presence I sat quiet and still. In my heart I heard His voice. "My dear child, I want you to think about the tears you've shed in your lifetime and what they've meant to you."

That did it! Tears trickled down my face, each one carrying a lifetime of emotions.

"Oh Lord, please. I don't want to cry. I'm so tired of crying."

"Lauren, don't you know that I am the author of your tears? Don't you know yet, that each of your tears has been a gift from your Heavenly Father?"

His words were kind, tender and compassionate. My tears began to feel warm and soothing. No longer were they unwelcome. It was one of those very priceless moments with the Father.

I picked up my pen. I couldn't wait a moment longer. It was time to write. "Dear Jesus, I love You, and I thank You for showing me the *blessing* of tears when I was feeling only their *anguish*." I went on to pray that the Holy Spirit would make me sensitive to His leading. "Let my pen and paper become Your writing tablet where You can write words that will bring blessing and encouragement to others."

Tears Are a Language

Chuck Swindoll expressed it so beautifully as he wrote, "When words fail, tears flow."[1]

There are more than 300,000 words in *Webster's Unabridged Dictionary*! One would think that there wasn't an emotion on earth that couldn't be adequately expressed through the endless vocabulary of written or spoken words.

And yet how often have we felt the sting of life's hurts so deeply that words seemed like meaningless articles of grammar, too superficial to even voice?

Several years ago, I was relaxing on the sofa watching a CBS "60 Minutes" segment about a young woman who had been adopted at birth. She was now in her twenties and was going to meet her birth mother for the first time. Being adopted myself, I had always thought in the back of my mind, "I wonder what it would be like to meet my real mother and father?" I sat glued to the TV screen.

The camera crew filmed her as she was being driven to her birth mother's home. I felt like I was in the car with her. I hung on to every word she said. No expression on her face went unnoticed.

I watched as the car drove up to a house and parked. The front door of the house and the back door of the car opened at the same time. An older woman walked out of the house, and the younger woman got out of the car. I found the suspense almost unbearable.

When they both suddenly broke into a run and held out their arms to embrace each other, I went on some sort of automatic pilot. I cannot explain it any other way. Without taking my eyes off the TV, I moved closer and closer to it. Within three or four seconds, I was face to face with the TV screen. I saw mother and daughter touch for the first time in their lives, their arms wrapped tightly around each other.

The daughter laid her head on her mother's shoulder and whispered, "Oh Mother, *my* mother!"

At that moment, from the deepest part of my being came a sound I had never heard before. It was not a word. It was just a sound—a deep, gut-wrenching groan. Then I wept, and I wept, and I wept.

Never had I dared to unlock the door to my own birth parents. I had always been too frightened to think about who or why or how or when. But on that Sunday evening, around 7 P.M., the door was yanked open with such force that the trauma all but consumed me.

After the "60 Minutes" segment was long over, I was still next to the TV. Tears were still spilling out like a swollen, rampaging river.

If anyone had asked me what I was feeling, I could not have responded. For there were no words in any language that could have begun to express what my heart and soul were feeling. Even I didn't know.

Yet through one unintelligible groan and a rush of tears, my body had said it all. It had found a "language of the soul," finally giving expression to burdens so heavy they couldn't be hidden any longer.

> When my mind couldn't say it,
> my heart cried it.
> My mind speaks words,
> but my heart speaks tears.

Words become barriers to communication when feelings are locked deeply within a wounded heart. The heart wants to speak, but the mind cannot form the thoughts into words. So the spirit of the heart takes over and says it all through tears.

It took me a long time to understand what had happened, and I never shared it with anyone. It was too personal, and I didn't know how to explain it without sounding a little "off-center." Then the Lord brought a few words from the Scriptures to mind as I considered that experience. I turned to Romans 8 and read verses 26 and 27.

> So too the [Holy] Spirit comes to our aid and bears us up in our weakness; for we do not know what prayer to offer nor how to offer it worthily as we ought, but the Spirit Himself goes to meet our supplication and pleads in our behalf with unspeakable yearnings and groanings too deep for utterance.
>
> And He Who searches the hearts of men knows what is in the mind of the [Holy] Spirit [what His intent is], because the Spirit intercedes and pleads [before God] in behalf of the saints according to and in harmony with God's will (AMP).

How do you feel after reading those verses? I feel ten feet tall! Why, I'm so precious to God that He has sent me

Someone to live within me who will listen to the language of my heart. And when my heart needs to talk to God, but I don't know how, the Holy Spirit pleads in my behalf with yearnings that are unspeakable and groanings that are too deep for words!

And what is true for me is true for you, too. The Holy Spirit is looking out for you. He's keeping watch over your heart. When it begins to get overstressed, overburdened, or in deep sorrow, so much so that it can't even express itself to God, the Holy Spirit takes over and says, "Child, don't worry! Let me pray for you. I have been listening to your heart, and I hear its hurt. God will listen to me, and He will understand what I am telling Him on your behalf."

Do you know, my friend, that you have a mediator, a go-between, an ambassador who represents you before the throne of God? He knows your thoughts and needs even better than you do. He volunteers to act on your behalf when you are at such a desperate or hurting place that you are not even certain which end is up.

The Holy Spirit, whom Jesus sent to be your comforter, will be that person to you.

I know beyond any doubt that my groan of anguish and the tears that I shed in front of that television set were a prayer from my heart. I believe that in my helplessness, the Holy Spirit took over for me and cried out to God in "unspeakable yearnings and groanings too deep for utterance."

Are you going through a difficulty in your own life at this moment? A situation so desperate that defeat seems inevitable? Are you at a breaking point? Do you feel helpless in trying to deal with the situation? Have you tried to pray, many times over, and you simply didn't have the words to say? Did you finally just give up and quit praying?

May I encourage you to let the tears flow. I encourage you to let the Holy Spirit take your tears to God, to present them to Him as the language of your heart. Let Him petition the Father on your behalf.

Chuck Swindoll says of tears, "A teardrop on earth summons the King of Heaven."[2] Your tears will never go unnoticed. They are as important as words—perhaps even more important! For they come out of the abundance of your heart, and they reach all the way to heaven.

Tears are not a sign of weakness, nor are they a childish display of emotions. Listen to what David wrote:

> You have seen me tossing and turning through the night. You have collected all my tears and preserved them in your bottle! You have recorded every one in your book (Psalm 56:8 TLB).

Your Father wastes none of your tears—not even one! Even though they may spill to the floor, He sees each one, and He tenderly recovers it as an offering of prayer from your heart unto His.

Jesus is sincerely moved by your troubles. Isaiah said about Jesus, "In all their affliction he was afflicted" (Isaiah 63:9 KJV). He weeps with you. He groans with you. His heart is heavy with yours. Did you know that the Scriptures never record that Jesus laughed? But more than once, they record that He was in tears.

Do you remember Jesus' reaction when He went with Mary to the tomb of Lazarus? Lazarus was a dear friend of Jesus'. His sister Mary had just fallen at Jesus' feet and cried, "Lord, if you had been here, my brother would not have died" (John 11:21 NIV).

Can you imagine the effect those words must have had on Jesus? Can you imagine how deeply it hurt Him to know that Lazarus' sister felt it was His fault? She thought that He had allowed Lazarus to die, because He hadn't arrived in time to heal him. What heaviness must have filled His heart!

Everyone, who by now had surrounded Jesus, was weeping. The Scripture records that "he was deeply moved" and that "he groaned in the spirit" (John 11:33 KJV). Perhaps one of the most profound and moving verses in the whole of the Scriptures follows in John 11:35 (NIV). It shows the humanity of Jesus. It shows the heart of Jesus, all in two simple words.

Jesus wept.

Was Jesus weeping because Lazarus had died and He had come too late? I don't think so. Surely Jesus knew that He had His Father's power to restore breath to the body that now lay lifeless and still. Why was it so important then, for John to record that Jesus wept?

It was important because it showed that Jesus was weeping for His *friend* Lazarus and not for the *man* Lazarus. The words, "Jesus wept," show that Jesus sorrowed; that He grieved over a dear friend's dying. They show that Jesus not only had the *capacity* to feel, but that He *did* feel, and furthermore, He chose to show His feelings through weeping. He was saying, "I am hurting, I am sorrowing. I am troubled."

I do not believe that those tears went unnoticed by His Father. They were a language all their own. Those tears were purposeful. I believe that Jesus communed with His Father through His tears.

Jesus was comforted through His tears.
His tears were cleansing.
His tears endeared Him to those about Him.

John 11:36 says that Lazarus' friends watched Jesus as He wept. "Behold how he loved him!" they commented. Even those who didn't know Jesus personally could understand the meaning of His tears.

If Jesus, the Son of God and the Savior of my soul, knew the value of tears and was not ashamed to let them freely come, why shouldn't I be like-minded? And why shouldn't you? Perhaps our tears will make us resemble our Lord more.

My Tears Are a Lovely Garden!

> They that sow in tears shall reap in joy (Psalm 126:5 KJV).

Shedding tears has never been a favorite pastime of mine, yet crying has taken up a good part of my past. For years, I felt like David when he lamented, "My tears have been my food day and night" (Psalm 42:3 NIV). I have wept so many tears that I have often made the remark, "I don't think anyone in the world has cried more than I have," and I have meant it sincerely. Buckets full; bushels full; tears enough to water the earth and fill the oceans! My tears were never-ending.

For over three years now, since the Lord has done such a beautiful work of healing, restoring and replacing those years that Satan took away from me, I have cried ever so much less. For the first time in my life, I have gone one month, two months, and maybe even longer without shedding a tear. It's been wonderful. I've been proud of it. In fact, one day I thought, *This is so neat, I'm going to ask the Lord to remove tears from my life forever. I don't ever want to cry again!*

So I asked the Lord just that, and I went for a long time with no tears. But something was missing. Something wasn't quite right, but I couldn't put my finger on it.

One Sunday, in church, we were singing a beautiful chorus about bowing before the Lord to worship Him. Suddenly my eyes filled with tears, and they began to run down my face. I didn't even have a tissue to wipe them away, since I had stopped bringing a supply of them to church with me long ago. I quickly tried to wipe them away with my hand without drawing attention to myself. But then something happened.

I realized that the tears felt good. I felt a release of emotions I had been keeping back, and I felt a cleansing of my heart. My spirit began to feel renewed. Since I was not able to keep the tears from coming and the only alternative was to walk out of the sanctuary, I chose to stay and let the tears flow. For the first time in my life, I began to appreciate tears.

Tears Are of Great Value

Later on that day, the Lord reminded me of the verse, "They that sow in tears shall reap in joy." I began to sense the great value and importance of tears—especially to the person who is hurting. A hurting person's tears are sown in pain. But they drop on tender soil, sown in the nurturing love of the Father.

Your tears become tiny little seeds that must be first shed and then sown, in order for them to begin to sprout into beautiful blossoms of joy! Your tears of pain, of sadness, of hurt, of bitterness and a host of other unwanted emotions give sprout to seeds of joy and hope and peace and forgiveness.

> Tears sown give birth to healing.
> Tears sown spring up as flowers of joy.
> Tears sown make your heart a lovely garden!

"Weeping may go on all night, but in the morning there is joy" (Psalm 30:5 TLB). Your weeping will not go on forever. There is an end to the sorrow. God promises to turn your sorrow into joy. He promises to water your seeds of tears, bringing life and joy to your heart of heaviness.

"When they walk through the Valley of Weeping it will become a place of springs where pools of blessing and refreshment collect after rains! They will grow constantly in strength and each of them is invited to meet with the Lord!" (Psalm 84:6,7 TLB).

Dear one, Jesus will turn your most painful and unwelcome tears, your Valley of Weeping, into a lovely garden of tears. Though they be sown in sorrow, they will sprout up as blessings. I have found this to be true. I have walked through the same valley in the same pain. If I were to walk with you through yours, together we would see your valley become "a place where pools of blessing and refreshment collect after rains."

A few months ago I went through a time of remembering and dealing with yet more of the rough times in my past. I was feeling discouraged and down on myself when my friend Vicki surprised me one morning with a lovely poem. A portion of it describes the tears she has seen me shed.

I ask that Jesus will minister His love to your hurt as you read my friend's thoughts about my tears.

> ... He stores up each tear and saves it to use
>   someday.
> You see, her very tears will water her own
>   garden. The garden called "Lauren" is full
>   of seeds. Waiting anxiously to peek their
>   tiny shoots out of the dark earth ...
> King Jesus has a lovely garden in her;
> and He sees all the flowers blooming,
> Radiant with color, full of fragrance,
> Altogether lovely.
> Jesus is speaking life to those seeds which
>   hide underneath the soil of hurt and pain ...

Those tears I have shed behind my smiles, those tears of pain, just like the ones you have shed, have been turned into a garden of beautiful colors and fragrances because Jesus has touched them.

God took tears that were so homely, and grew a thing of beauty from them—my very own rose garden. My garden is growing more beautiful every day. I see new colors. I smell new fragrances. Even though there are still painful times of tears, I've learned to let them come.

Restore Me, Lord

> I will...transform her Valley of Troubles
> into a door of hope (Hosea 2:15 TLB).

Tears are a recovery room for restoration. *Your tears will never be more than Jesus can use to bring you back to wholeness!* They will never drown your heart. They will never be without end!

I wish I could share with you every letter that I have received from a deeply hurting person who has written, "I need to cry so badly. But I'm afraid to, because I know I'll never be able to stop!" I read that so often that I could easily begin to let the tragedy of that expression pass me by. I have to stop and pray,

"God, don't ever let me forget when I was there!"

I do know how victims of hurt fear opening themselves up to tears. And I know that the one step that often brings initial healing and restoration is the step the hurting person fears the most. Tears shed over a deeply buried hurt can be so agonizingly painful that we may sometimes even feel physical pain.

In spite of the fear that "I'll never ever stop crying if I begin," I encourage you who are holding back a flood of tears to let them come. It could be a trickle. It could all rush out in an unchecked torrent. It could be accompanied with sobs and groanings. But in order that God will to be able to use your tears to cleanse and relieve your burdened heart, I plead with you, "Let go, and let the tears come!"

"But will I ever laugh again?" you ask.

Oh, yes! Yes, you will! God will turn those tears that you have given to Him into laughter. Psalm 39:13 says, "Let me recover and be filled with happiness again" (TLB). The recovery room of tears will effect the restoration of laughter and joy.

In *Satan's Underground* I wrote about one of the gifts Jesus has given to me that I thought I would never have: the gift of laughter. Wouldn't you know that laughing is one of the most abundant things I do now? I can laugh until my sides ache. I laugh until tears of joy run down my cheeks! Jesus has grown *tears of joy* from my *tears of pain*. Maybe that's why I can laugh so heartily now— because I have wept so deeply.

Yes, you who weep now will be rewarded with joy. The *absence* of tears does not mean the *presence* of joy, but the *shedding* of tears promises the *hope* of joy. Jesus speaks that promise to you when He says, "What happiness there is for you who weep, for the time will come when you shall laugh with joy!" (Luke 6:21 TLB).

To the one who is hurting now, those words may almost seem a little cruel, almost hurtful in themselves. It's hard to hear about laughter and joy in the intense heat of pain. But I promise you, Jesus did not say those words to taunt you or to tease you. They are not a cruel joke. They are the uncompromising, irrevocable truth of the living God who is saying to you, "I give you my Word, that you who weep now will laugh again! I give you my Word that you who sow a garden of tears will reap a garden of joy!"

I have never learned to enjoy tears. Crying is hard. Weeping is harder. To put it the way I feel it, "It's no fun! I'd rather not cry, thank you!" But I can tell you that I have learned the *value* of tears. I have felt the *healing* of tears. I have had the privilege of *sharing* another person's tears.

I saved the best thing about tears for the last. I can say it no better than the Lord's beloved disciple, John, who wrote in Revelation 21:4:

> And God shall wipe away all tears from their eyes; and there shall be no more death, neither sorrow, nor crying, neither shall there be any more pain: for the former things are passed away (KJV).

– 9 –

Touch Me,
Heal Me

◆

The shoe salesman walked toward me with arms opened wide. Panic! Fear! What's going on? Should I run? No, I can't. Customers are watching.

Now he is in front of me. Two arms reach out and give me a big hug. Then he steps back and grins at me from ear to ear. "That's one for the hug therapist," he says proudly.

Suddenly it dawns on me. I'm wearing one of my favorite shirts. On the front are the words, "HUG THERAPIST." Below the words is a picture of a contented bear with arms and paws wrapped around, giving himself a big bear hug.

Now I understand. Panic's gone. Fear's gone. And I think it's terrific that a total stranger was so unashamed and confident in himself that he could respond to me as a "Hug Therapist." No, I am not a therapist, but I sure have learned to enjoy both giving and receiving hugs!

My advice to anyone who likes both to give and receive hugs is to get a T-shirt that says something like "I Like Hugs!" Believe me, you will be in for some heartwarming experiences!

I do want to make a couple of necessary qualifications before we go any further. Touching may not be for everyone. Although I am a devoted fan of hugging, I realize that there are those who, for their own reasons, don't like to touch or to be touched.

There are also those who believe that the sole purpose for hugging is to build a physically intimate relationship. I am not talking about this kind of touching. I am talking about the good, old-fashioned therapeutic hugs that almost everybody needs—hugs that say "from one human being to another, I care about you. I just wanted you to know." This kind of hugging touches the heart and in no way is related to sexuality.

Of course, one must be careful that hugs and touches are given and received for the right reasons. They should be from a heart filled with Christian love and warmth— caring, compassionate and comforting. They must never be threatening, frightening or forced, but given with respect to the receiver's sensitivities. Just as the gift of touch is important, so is the acceptance of touch equally important.

The Lost Art

Sometimes touching seems to be a lost art. Holding and hugging are becoming endangered species. In a world where so many people are hurting, the enemy is winning by putting up barriers to hinder people from touching each other.

"It's sissy to show affection."

"What will others think?"

"Someone else might misinterpret my hug."

"What if I'm rejected by the 'huggee'?"

And between people of the same sex:

"Someone might think I'm...you know!"

Satan certainly does his best to wipe out one of the most effective and essential ways of bringing comfort and healing to a hurting person! Let's look at a common situation where the communication of touch is all-important. Linda is saying, "I know Suzie is hurting. I would sure like to give her a hug, but I don't know if I should. She might not like it."

Suzie is saying, "I feel so alone. I wish someone would show me that they love me. I sure wish Linda would just give me a hug, but I'm afraid to ask her." And so Linda keeps the gift the Lord wanted her to give Suzie. And Suzie never asks for the gift she so desperately needs. Both the giver and the receiver have lost out on a blessing.

Or, consider this scenario. Tom and Becky's marriage is in trouble. Both have hurt each other so badly that they fear their marriage is almost irreparable. In desperation, they agree to get help.

Tom

Tom finally works up the nerve to talk to his best friend, Rod. He tells Rod the worst of the worst. He really opens up the dark and hidden areas of his marriage. It all comes spilling out in shades of *black* and *blacker*. It's so awful that he begins to feel emotions he didn't even know were there.

Tears begin to fill his eyes. That is a new experience. He is ashamed and fights them back with fierce determination.

Rod notices the tears in Tom's eyes. "Hey brother, get hold of yourself!" he says assertively. "Be a man! God wants you to be strong. You can make it, man. I have faith in you. You're not a quitter. You're like me. We're both fighters! Don't let it get to you."

Even though Tom feels like wilting lower and lower in his chair, he valiantly tries to assume the strong posture of confidence he knows Rod expects of him. Trying to keep his voice from breaking, he asks, "Rod, would you pray for Becky and me?"

"Sure thing, Tom." They bow their heads. While their eyes are closed, Tom brushes a tear from his cheek with the back of his hand, hoping Rod doesn't notice.

"Dear God," Rod begins, "Tom's marriage is in trouble. Help him to be the strong man You expect him to be. We're asking You to heal his marriage. Amen."

Tom and Rod say goodbye. As Tom drives home his heart hurts worse than ever. Feeling the tears come so close to the surface, yet having to hold them back, makes him feel like he's going to burst with pain. He drives into his garage feeling frustrated and angry.

Becky

In the meantime, Becky has phoned her best friend, Marsha. "Marsha, I've got to talk to you."

Marsha hears the urgency in Becky's voice and says, "I'll be right over. My mom will watch the kids. Can you hang on until I get there?" she asks, her voice filled with concern.

"Yes, I'm all right. I just need to talk. I've put it off too long. I can't wait any longer."

When Marsha arrives, Becky seems apprehensive. "Hon, come over here and sit where I can be close to you," Marsha gently urges.

Marsha puts her arms around Becky's shoulders and gives a gentle squeeze, pulling her a little closer. "I've never seen you so tense, Becky. Can you tell me what's wrong?"

Becky bows her head. Her hands are clasped tightly together. Marsha covers them with her hand. "Talk to me, Becky. You know you can tell me anything."

No sooner has Marsha spoken than Becky's tears begin to cascade down her face. Marsha takes her hand off Becky's long enough to pull tissue from the box on the coffee table. She begins to gently wipe the tears from Becky's face.

"You know, hon, Jesus sees your tears. He says that He collects them in a bottle. They are precious in His sight, Becky. Don't be afraid to let them loose."

At that moment Becky breaks. She lays her head on Marsha's shoulder and begins to sob. The sobs grow louder and the tears multiply. Her cries come from a deeply-wounded heart that she valiantly had fought to keep secret for so long.

"Jesus loves you, Becky. And I love you. Whatever's wrong, we're here for you," Marsha whispers compassionately. She kisses her on the forehead and then she holds her for a long time. There is no talking and no praying, at least out loud.

But Marsha is praying silently all the while, asking God to use her as a channel through which He can minister His healing. The tension begins to leave. The tears grow less. The sobbing quiets. The painful hurts begin to form into words that tell a story of unfaithfulness on both sides of the marriage. It is a tragic story of denial, of accusations, of each blaming the other for failure, of shattered dreams.

Marsha remains silent, giving Becky an "I'm here with you" squeeze every so often.

When the wounds of Becky's heart are finally opened to the healing love of Jesus, she begins to feel a warmth that she hadn't felt for a long time.

Becky follows Marsha to the kitchen as she begins to make coffee for them. "Becky," Marsha asks softly, "how are you feeling?"

Becky takes a deep breath and heaves a sigh. "Oh Marsha, I feel like I've been touched by the hands of Jesus! I can't remember the last time I was held like that." Becky's eyes, already reddened, become moist again, but this time Marsha notices a look of contentment in them.

"I've felt so unloved, so cold. It's almost like I've been living in a vacuum." Becky pauses for a moment, enjoying the fragrance of the brewing coffee. "You know, when you put your arm around me and I laid my head on your shoulder, I felt that emptiness begin to leave. I knew you were praying for me, and I felt God ministering to me through you."

After Marsha pours their coffee, they sit down at the kitchen table and have a short time of prayer, this time out loud. And they read some of their favorite passages in the Book of Psalms.

Marsha finally gives Becky one last hug and leaves. Becky finally hears Tom drive into the garage. She's ready to meet him. But Tom is not ready to meet her!

What Makes the Difference?

Tom and Becky had both asked for help. They were both sincere. They both prayed. But one was given the touch of love, and one was denied it.

Oh sure, I know all-too-well that it isn't "macho" for men to put an arm around each other, let alone sustain that show of love and concern for more than two seconds. I know it's thought to be a sign of weakness when men cry. I know that men are instilled from the time they are little boys to not show their real emotions—especially the emotions of hurt. And a lot of men would be proud of Tom, because Tom "acted like a man" in the midst of his troubles.

Let's get real! Tom's emptiness needed to be filled. His tears needed to be allowed to come. His hurt needed to be touched. To believe that tears, holding, touching, and hugging are not acceptable or appropriate is erroneous. More importantly, it is depriving people who are hurting of the channel through which God may be choosing to accomplish a healing in them.

A pat on the back. A hand on the knee. An arm on the

shoulder. An offered handkerchief that silently says, "It's okay if you cry." These are the very acts through which God ministers His healing. If Rod had given Tom the human touch of compassion, Tom would more than likely have broken wide open.

When a compassionate touch knocks on the heart's door, there is nearly always a response. Even when the door has long been bolted shut, a touch, a hug, an embrace or even a pat on the hand does wonders in turning the key. It may open just a crack at first, but it will open!

Who Doesn't Need to Be Touched?

In most cases, a person who says, either in words or in body language, "Don't touch me!" is a person who has been hurt deeply by another person. The "wall" is a means of protection against further hurt.

Usually that person needs the touch of another human more than anyone else!

A touch is warm. A hug feels good. A shoulder to cry on is comforting. There is just something about physical contact that brings healing. Maybe that's why Satan does his best to get victims to wall up their hurt with a barrier so thick that it is almost impenetrable. Barriers such as:

- ✦ I don't need anyone.
- ✦ I don't trust anyone.
- ✦ How do I know you won't hurt me too?
- ✦ Touching scares me, because it makes me get in touch with my feelings. And I don't want to feel!

Meanwhile, deep on the inside, far from where the enemy's voice can reach, there comes a faint cry.

- ✦ If someone would just hold me.
- ✦ I'll die if someone doesn't give me a hug.
- ✦ Is there no one to put their arms around me?

Such was the cry of a desperately hurting person who wrote me recently saying, "I need to find one person who will love me, hold me and be there for me." And, as you who hurt know, it is seldom enough to just hear the words, "Trust Jesus. He is always there."

It's not that we wouldn't trust Jesus. It's not that He's unavailable. Jesus is our source of healing. But when it comes to the needs of others, *we* are His arms. *We* are His hands. He reaches out to the hurting through the touch of human beings. He uses our arms and hands to show His compassion to a hurting world.

Touch Brings Life

Science has proven that an infant will die eventually if it is not touched. It may be fed and otherwise tended to mechanically. But if that little body does not feel the touch of a human hand, the body will feel that it is not being cared for. Scientists have shown that one of the human body's most powerful needs is touching through human contact.

The unfulfillment of this powerful need is called "touch deprivation." Just as the harmfulness of light deprivation was discussed in an earlier chapter, of equal significance is the lack of touching to human health.

What is so vital about a touch? Is it merely that one layer of skin rests on another layer of skin? I don't think so. When I am touched, it isn't my skin that says, "I am loved." No. It's my heart! When science has proven that even an infant needs human touch, why wouldn't all men and women, boys and girls share the same need?

There is no one of any age or gender who doesn't need to feel the touch of love. And if I am a Christian, how much more should I be seeking out the hurting who are crying out for the touch that heals?

Tighter Than a Drum

I had the privilege of getting to know a woman who is a prime example of the radical change that touch can produce in a human life. She was introduced to me through a mutual friend.

She had been both physically and sexually abused for several years as a young child. Her undisclosed and undealt-with trauma closed her emotions tighter than a drum.

As you know by now, I'm a hugger! I hug anyone who will let me get close to them. Perhaps one of my ways of getting hugs is to give them. At any rate, I go on an automatic hugging mode, or at least a touching mode, when I meet someone. I feel like I haven't really communicated with them unless I have touched them.

When my friend introduced me to this woman, I put out my arms to give her a hug. No way! Red flags and warning signs announced loudly and clearly, "DO NOT TOUCH!" She ducked to avoid my arms and took at least two steps backward.

I instantly knew that I had overstepped my boundaries. I had taken a liberty with her that I shouldn't have, knowing she was an abuse victim. "I'm sorry," I apologized. "Please forgive me. I just feel for you, and I want you to know I care for you. My reaching to hug you was my way of letting you know that."

I saw her almost weekly for several weeks. Only once was I not thinking, and I reached out to put my hands on hers as I told her that I had been praying for her. She quickly withdrew her hand and put it behind her back.

About three months later our mutual friend told me that this woman had a surprise for me. I must have looked puzzled, and asked, "What's that?"

I found out the next time I saw our friend.

I think I saw her smile for the first time. What a beautiful sight—a grin on the face of someone who had just recently been waiting to die. This woman had been courting death for several years.

"Wow! You look like a different person!" I told her excitedly.

"That's not the surprise," she said with a gleam in her eyes.

"That's not it?" I asked. "Well, what is it? Lay it on me!"

To my amazement and thrill she unhesitatingly reached out her arms and wrapped them around me. Was I ever blessed! "I can hug you now...and you can hug me," she said happily. "And you know something, Lauren?"

"What?" I asked. I could hardly wait for her answer. I didn't think I could stand another surprise. She had already overwhelmed me.

"It feels really good!" she exclaimed.

"You know what, my friend?" I asked. "It felt really good to me, too! I needed your hug!"

Have you closed your heart as tight as a drum? And yet all the while, are you wanting to be touched, to be hugged, to be held, to feel the love of another person?

How I encourage you to reach out in your need. Learn to receive from others who are the arms and hands of a loving Father. All through the Gospels of Matthew, Mark, Luke and John, Jesus is reaching out to touch those in need. And those in need are reaching out to touch Him.

> As many as touched him were made whole
> (Mark 6:56 KJV).

My Friend, the Cop

I cannot end without sharing a story about Dennis

Adams, a police sergeant and my security guard at a recent seminar.

When he was first introduced to me, he immediately asked me for a hug. His warmth was unexpected, and he must have sensed my bewilderment because he immediately told me a story that I will never forget. It happened one very lonely night on a faraway hill in Vietnam called "Muther's Ridge."

"There had been intense fighting. Every one of my buddies was killed," he began. "I looked around and saw them all shot up and lifeless."

About then I mustered up the nerve to look into his face. Tears had quickly filled his eyes, and as he continued his recounting, his voice began to break.

"When you're a Marine machine gunner, no matter what happens, you're not supposed to express your feelings. If your buddy was killed, you just adopted the 'better him than me' attitude.

"But I was only nineteen years old and as I crouched in my foxhole I was scared, lonely and wanting a hug from my mom, my dad, my brother—anybody. I felt like I was the last person on earth. I cried out, 'Oh God, I need someone to hold onto!'

"But it was just me and my M-60 machine gun. I had never been more alone in my life. Being a big, tough Marine in Vietnam I couldn't say anything, so I picked up my gun and hugged it instead, holding it close to my heart." Dennis' eyes were reddened by then, and a few tears were trickling down his cheeks.

I was so moved with compassion that I wasn't sure just how to respond. *If I give him a hug*, I thought to myself, *I'll lose it. I'll just fall apart.*

In a few seconds Dennis gained enough composure to go on. "When I found out that you were coming here to participate in a seminar on satanism, and I was going to be your bodyguard, I bought your book. I had no idea what I was in for!

"Your story brought back the memory of the loneliest day of my life, a memory that up till now I had successfully managed to block out of my mind—the massacre on Muther's Ridge.

"When I got to the page where you shared about being so lonely that you felt like going outside and hugging a telephone pole, I just broke. At that moment I had to deal with my hurt that I had buried for twenty years. I cried for the first time since that lonely day I sat on that hill in Nam."

What Dennis said to me next went right to the core of one of my deepest hurts. "Lauren, I hurt so much for the little girl you wrote about because I too knew that lonely and desperate feeling. That was when I decided that if and when we ever met I was going to ask for a hug."

Stopping for a moment to wipe his eyes, he continued in a broken voice. "If you hadn't written your book, then I would never have been set free from my pain. I would never have been able to know the relief of sharing a hug with you."

The little girl in me was still hurting. I had never been able to hold and hug her, and I certainly had never allowed anyone else to. Why, no one else even knew she existed until I dared to take the first scary step of sharing her in the book. And now, here was a grown man (a policeman no less!) who was asking for permission to hug the lonely and hurting little girl inside me!

The *adult* Lauren was saying, "No way, man! No one is ever going to touch that little girl!" At the same time, I felt the little girl crying out, "Please hold me."

To my disbelief I heard myself saying, "Sure, you can have a hug." And somehow I felt my arms reaching out to him.

I was so lost in my own world of thoughts that I barely heard Dennis as he released his hug. "Lauren, that hug we gave each other was for that little girl who wanted a hug so badly. And it was from a nineteen-year-old who was a scared and lonely Marine in Vietnam."

It wasn't until several months later that I told Dennis that his hug was the beginning of a long period of healing to the little girl in me. That healing process, started by a touch and a hug, is still continuing.

Dennis and I are both being healed.

> Joy and hope have ebbed away
> I cannot face tomorrow, much less today
> So hug me with your words
> Put Your arms under mine
> Hold me tight until I'm fine.[1]

I encourage you to offer the healing touch of Jesus to one another.

– 10 –

God, Don't Ask Me to Be a Job!

◆

Job was sitting in his favorite rocking chair after a long, hard day. He was ready to relax. The sun was beginning to set in the west, casting hues of orange across the vast expanse of land that stretched in every direction as far as the eye could see. It all belonged to Job. God had surely rewarded him richly for his faithfulness!

The fruits of Job's labors were many: 7 sons; 3 daughters; 7,000 sheep; 3,000 camels; 500 teams of oxen; 500 donkeys; and many servants. He was the richest cattleman in the entire area.

Job's wife sat down alongside him. A smile of pleasure spread across her face. "You know, God has blessed us with such good children. I think we must be the most blessed family anywhere." She beamed, her face radiating the joy of a contented wife and mother.

"You're right, honey," he replied. "God has given us everything we asked Him for. I'd feel embarrassed to ask for more!"

As Job stretched out his legs, he sighed with contentment. "You and I have good health. Our kids are responsible and married. Our servants are devoted to us. What more could we want, honey?"

His wife looked at him thoughtfully. "Sometimes it almost seems too good to be true, doesn't it? Do you ever

get to wondering what it would be like if we lost everything? What would we do? I shouldn't want our kids to
have to provide for us. And I worry about the grandkids.
What if one of them got sick and died? We've never had
to go through anything like that."

She stopped suddenly and took a deep breath. "You
know," she said softly, carefully choosing her words, "it's
almost as if a fear . . . a fear of losing everything we've
worked for . . . comes over me. I'm getting so paranoid
that I'm afraid if I say it any louder Satan might hear
me."

"Well, honey," Job answered, repositioning himself so
he could speak to her face-to-face, "what difference
would it make if he did hear you? Don't you know that he
can't touch us? We've given everything we have to God.
It all belongs to Him."

The idea of losing everything—his spacious home, his
vast landholdings and all his livestock—sounded so pre-
posterous that he began to chuckle. With a twinkle in
his eyes he put his arms around his wife, "Come on,
honey! You've got to know that Satan can't get within
ten feet of us!"

Job felt her shaking and he suddenly realized that
this was no joking matter as far as she was concerned.
Her fear was very real.

"I didn't mean to make light of what you're feeling,
hon. I'm sorry. It's just that I know God has His angels
surrounding us," he said confidently, trying very hard to
reassure her. "And you know He loves us."

Putting his hand on the railing as he watched the last
rays of the sun slip behind the hills, Job announced
assuredly, "None of us knows how long we have on the
earth. But I believe that as long as we have life and
breath to serve the Lord, nothing is going to happen to
us."

Fiction? Maybe. But the story of Job's life that follows is all-too-true. We wish we didn't know it. We wish it hadn't happened. How could it be that a man who feared God, a man who was honest and upright in his dealings, would suffer such doom? Could Job have been mistaken to trust his life, his family and his possessions to the divine providence of God?

Not long after that imaginary conversation Job's losses begin to read like front-page headlines:

Thieves Steal Job's Cattle and Murder His Servants

Fire Destroys Job's Property

Windstorm Collapses Home— All of Job's Children Dead

How could Job have been so wrong? Was he only fooling himself into entrusting his worldly goods to the keeping of God? Was his trust totally unfounded? It's hard to imagine anyone having such faith in the Lord. At first, even the loss of family and possessions didn't cause Job to cry out to God, "This isn't fair!"

The Scriptures say that Job "fell to the ground in worship and said: Naked I came from my mother's womb, and naked I will depart. The Lord gave and the Lord has taken away; may the name of the Lord be praised" (Job 1:21 NIV).

As if Job's attitude wasn't unusual enough when he said, "May the name of the Lord be praised," read the verse that follows: "In all this, Job did not sin by charging God with wrongdoing" (Job 1:22 NIV).

What trust! What faith! Total and unswerving faith. Could anything shake Job? It certainly didn't seem so. Ah, but Job's story doesn't end there. Would to God that it did!

Satan, as usual, was being a sore loser. He just wasn't satisfied with destroying all of Job's wealth down to his very family. I bet it really got under his skin that Job was still worshiping and praising God. That was just too much for Satan to handle!

Job 2:2 tells us that Satan came to the Lord. When the Lord asked him where he had been, he answered, "Roaming through the earth and going back and forth in it."

He probably had been pacing up and down muttering to himself about his failure to get Job to curse God. I can imagine him saying, "What do I have to do to this self-righteous man? I guess I could kill him, but then I would never find out if he would have turned his back on God. I know. I'll make him so sick that he will wish he were dead!"

And so the agreement was sealed between the Lord and Satan with one condition only—Satan could do anything he wanted to Job except take his life.

Can't you picture Satan rubbing his hands together in glee and anticipation? The thing that probably pleased him most was that Job would think that his beloved Lord was afflicting him, not the devil. If he could pull that deception off, what a coup it would be!

Then the enemy came up with a really good one. He inflicted Job with a grievous case of boils. "We'll just see how strong the old boy's faith is now," he must have snickered to himself.

So Job was sorely afflicted with boils. Some scholars are of the opinion that Job's disease was of an acute nature, with symptoms that included an extremely painful and feverish inflammation of the skin.

He even managed to use Job's wife to taunt him. I can picture "I told you so" written all over her face. She was one who could love the Lord in the good times, but when the things she held dear were taken from her, she couldn't withstand the loss. Her first impulse was to blame God for the troubles. Scoffingly, she chided him: "Are you still trying to be godly when God has done all this to you? Curse him and die" (Job 2:9 TLB).

Well, any one of us would be tempted to have the same attitude, to curse God and wish to die! One would think that Job's obvious reply to his wife would have been, "You're right, honey. God has been unfair to me. I would be better off dead."

Not Job! Job's faith in a righteous God was still strong. His response to her mirrored his faith. "Shall we accept good from God, and not trouble?" Then we read once again, "In all this, Job did not sin in what he said" (Job 2:10 NIV).

Defeat number two for Satan. His plot against Job was crushed.

Job Is Human After All

After seven days and seven nights of sitting on the ground scattered with ashes and listening to his friends weep because of his sorry state, Job broke. If the Scriptures had not recorded that, I'm not sure that his story would even be believable, or that it would encourage others who are in dire straits.

These are the facts: Job lived a godly life. He had loved and served the Lord. He had raised his family in the way of righteousness. He had done no wrong equal to his affliction. Yet he was suddenly overcome in a desperate trial. It is for these very reasons that you and I can take comfort and encouragement when such trials overcome us.

I, myself, have read and reread the Book of Job many times over because I so desperately have needed to be reassured that, since Job went through great affliction and was delivered and restored to health and prosperity, I too can also make it. I can be carried through my distress by the same grace that Job was given, and I can be comforted with the same comfort as Job received.

One can look at Job's plight and come to one of three conclusions:

1) Job did nothing to deserve his trial. Therefore it was unfair that God allowed Satan to afflict him sorely.

2) Job had committed a secret sin and his affliction was sent as a punishment from God.

3) Job was a mortal man, subject to trials and afflictions of this world. He was not exempt from the tragedies of life just because He loved and served God.

In our humanness, we are prone to choose the first conclusion. If I am to be honest with you, I must admit that, in the midst of my darkest trials, I've thought that God was unfair. I've thought, *I didn't deserve this*; and that *Mrs. Jones, who isn't any better than I am, isn't going through anything near what I am going through. So why am I having to go through it?*

Using common sense (though I find it much more tempting to follow my feelings!), I know that we live in a world where Satan is still very much alive and well, and just because we are Christians, we are not exempt from earthly ills. The one promise we can stand upon, however, is that God will be faithful to be with us in the midst of our affliction and that He will bring us out of our affliction in His time. *Of that I am sure!*

Job followed this line of reasoning for as long as he could, but he finally succumbed to acting like all the rest of us have acted in our most unwanted circumstances. Does Job's lamenting sound familiar? Listen to him talk to God:

I am weary of living. Let me complain freely.
I will speak in my sorrow and bitterness. Does
it really seem right to you to oppress and
despise me? I will say to God, "Don't just condemn me—tell me why you are doing it!" You
have made me, and yet you destroy me.

Your real motive in making me was to destroy me if I sinned; and to refuse to forgive my
iniquity. Just the slightest wickedness and I
am done for (Job 10:1,3,2,8,13-15 TLB).

Can you identify with Job? I don't think there are
many of us who can't. And Job isn't finished yet. He's got
a lot more to complain about. He adds pity upon pity
when he gives one of the most sorrowful laments a man
in despair could cry:

If I'm good, that doesn't count. . . . If I start to
get up off the ground, you leap on me like a lion
and quickly finish me off.

Oh, that my sadness and troubles were
weighed. For they are heavier than the sand of
a thousand seashores. For the Lord has struck
me down with his arrows; he has sent his
poisoned arrows deep within my heart. All
God's terrors are arrayed against me (Job
10:15,16; 6:1-4 TLB).

Finally Job gets down to the bottom line. He can go
no lower in his despair when he cries out from his
gut-wrenched feelings: "Why then did you even let me
be born? Why didn't you let me die at birth? Then I
would have been spared this miserable experience" (Job
10:18,19 TLB).

Not only did Job want to die by now, he wished that he
had never been born! That's the ultimate bitterness
against God: to question God's wisdom in creating him
in the first place.

I like Job. A kindred spirit is he!

He lives an upright life. Everything is taken away, even his health. He holds onto his unswerving faith in God as long as he can. But...

Job Finally Crashes!

He complains. He doubts the fairness of God. He wants to die. This is a common pattern for people in pain, and it shouldn't make anyone feel ashamed or guilty. It is honest. Realistic. Human!

Job was so miserable and depressed that he couldn't have pretended nor put on a mask even if he had wanted to. If Job and the psalmist, David, had been neighbors, they surely would have had a lot to commiserate about. Both knew the highest joys in the Lord and the lowest valleys in sorrow. Both sat on the mountaintop of victory only to plummet to the lowest chasm of defeat. Listening to Job and David's lamenting, it's difficult to tell them apart. You have just heard Job's cries. Now listen to David's. David is observing the ways of the wicked and how they can only but seem to prosper in them.

He complains:

> All through life their road is smooth! They grow sleek and fat. They aren't always in trouble and plagued with problems like everyone else.... These fat cats have everything their hearts could ever wish for! (Psalm 73:4-7 TLB).

I love it! At first glance, how true! Then David gets down to the thing that's really bothering him. It isn't the *wicked man's prosperity*. It is *his own* (the righteous man's) *lack of prosperity*. He continues:

> Have I been wasting my time? Why take the trouble to be pure? All I get out of it is trouble

and woe—every day and all day long! (Psalm
73:13,14 TLB).

Both Job and David are saying, "I've been good. Where
has it gotten me? I'm getting more miserable while
those less-deserving souls are getting fatter! Where is
the justice of it all? Where is the fairness of God?"

We Are All Asking

Letters come to me every day asking the same questions. I hear the voices of broken hearts on the phone
asking: "Why did it happen to me?"; "What did I do to
deserve this?"; "What good does it do to serve God?"

I wish I had all the answers, but I don't. I can only
share with you some thoughts the Lord has given to
encourage me along the way. These concepts have enabled me to keep my faith and trust in Him even when I
wasn't given a definitive answer to my "whys."

In recent years, a complex and life-threatening blood
disorder has put me in the hospital often and for extended periods of time. My illness placed me in an ir-
resistible position for some Christians to offer their
"reasons" for my illness.

I'll never forget one phone call I received from a volun-
teer worker of a youth ministry. I had never spoken to
this man before. I hadn't even heard of him. A friend of
mine had asked him to call me, because she felt his
prayers might be an encouragement to me.

I must admit that my spirits were dragging the floor,
and a few kind words might have kept them from being
stepped on!

The phone rang. When one is in a hospital bed, the
phone is always in the wrong place! Taking hold of the
trapeze bar, I groaned as I pulled myself to the other side
of the bed. My arm had to reach through IV tubings, an
oxygen line and then in between the water pitcher and a

vase of flowers. Finally, my hand found the phone. I was already exhausted. I remember thinking, *This better be good!*

"Hello," I answered breathlessly. (I've forgotten his name, but I'll call him "Jim.")

"Hello, Lauren. My name is Jim. You don't know me, but I've heard about you, and I feel the Lord has a word for you."

To be truthful, I have always been a little uneasy when someone tells me that. Unless I have been deliberately shutting my ears to the Lord's voice, I have always thought, *Why didn't the Lord tell me?*

But, since I know that the Lord does speak through other people, I acquiesced against my better judgment and listened to Jim without interrupting.

"Lauren, do you want to be healed?" The voice was very serious.

I thought, *Uh-oh. I know what's coming next.* Just to be stubborn, I wanted to say, "No. I love being in pain!" I controlled that urge, however, and managed to respond, "Yes, I do. Very much."

"Well, the choice is yours," he said matter-of-factly. "Sickness in a Christian's life is sent by God because of unconfessed sin." His voice was not only serious, but downright stern.

Jim continued, unfortunately. (You may be sensing that I was having an attitude problem. You're right.) "All you have to do is confess and repent of your sin, and God will heal you. It's that simple. It's your choice."

The only words I appreciated from him were his last ones. "I'm going to hang up now, because I can't make the choice for you. Goodbye, and God bless you." The next sound I heard was the dial tone.

Yes, I know. I should have shrugged it off and heaved a sigh of relief. But I couldn't. His words hurt, really hurt! When someone is in pain, another's insensitivity, no matter how well-meaning, often hurts twice as badly.

Tears filled my eyes and soon ran down my face. I had to take out the oxygen tube so I could blow my nose. And once again, as I had done countless times before, I asked the Lord if there might be any secret sin that I wasn't aware of, and if so, to forgive me!

It was some consolation to realize that Job went through this very same experience with his friends. Their logic progressed like this:

1) God makes the righteous happy.

2) He makes sinners miserable.

3) Job is miserable.

4) Therefore, Job must have committed some sin.

5) The solution for him is to repent.

6) If he does, God will forgive him and take away the pain.[1]

What an oversimplification! It is true that we sometimes find ourselves in dire straits because of sin. The drug addict can pay a heavy penalty for his use of drugs. The morally-loose person may well reap the penalty of death with the onset of AIDS. The alcoholic mother who neglects or abuses her children may have her children taken from her. The office worker who is late to work day after day may find a "final notice" in his box.

We do reap what we sow.

What is *not true* is the conclusion that all suffering is due to sin in our lives. What *is not* true is the conclusion that if we are not delivered from our suffering immediately, we have *chosen* to not be delivered. Those beliefs are not only erroneous, but can be devastating to the person who is suffering.

If my suffering *is* indeed because of sin, I know what

to do. If my suffering *is not* because of sin, what is the answer?

I Encourage You in Your Suffering

One of the Scriptures the Lord has used in my life is 1 Peter 1:6,7:

> Now for a little while you may have had to suffer grief in all kinds of trials. These have come so that your faith—of greater worth than gold, which perishes even though refined by fire—may be proved genuine and may result in praise, glory and honor... (NIV).

Jesus says to me, "Lauren, the trial of your faith is much more precious than the refinement of gold. As gold is the most precious of metals, so is your faith one of the most precious of Christian attributes. Gold will eventually evaporate in the hottest flame, but faith will increase as the fire grows more intense. Gold will perish in the end. Your faith will last you forever until it brings you into the heavenlies when you meet Jesus."

The trial of my faith will only make me stronger, even if by fire! We can rejoice in our trials when we know that God is perfecting an eternal work in us. God's design in allowing us to suffer is not for our *destruction*, but rather for our *strengthening*!

The one truth that is sometimes a hard pill to swallow is that we do have a choice in whether we allow Satan to destroy us or whether we allow God to strengthen us through our trials.

Job began to wilt under the trial of his faith. Considering the utter destruction of his life, is there any one of us who wouldn't have done likewise?

But in a few moments, we'll see that Job began a journey back in the right direction.

Another truth in which I have taken great comfort is that no one will ultimately lose by trusting God. I can never go wrong in choosing to place my faith in God. Yes, even when I don't understand. Even when I can't see. Even when my faith is weak and as small as a grain of sand. I cannot lose in God!

I trust my life to God in His promise:

> I placed the sand for the boundary of the sea, a perpetual barrier beyond which it cannot pass and by an everlasting ordinance beyond which it cannot go. And though the waves of the sea toss and shake themselves, yet they cannot prevail [against the feeble grains of sand which God has ordained by nature to be sufficient for His purpose]; though the [billows] roar yet they cannot pass over that [barrier] (Jeremiah 5:22 AMP).

If the tides were not checked, the entire earth would be submerged. But God is in control. What a comfort and encouragement! *God has placed boundaries around our lives beyond which no trials can pass!* And though those trials pound like waves against that barrier, they cannot overwhelm our souls.

There is always a point where God says, "Enough! My child has had enough." And though the billows may continue to roll like an angry sea and threaten to sweep over us, they will not prevail. If there is one thing that I have heard God say to me through the Book of Job, it is to absolutely trust in His divine providence.

Let God Be God, For He Is in Control

When our circumstances are shouting, "Hey, what's going on here? Where is God? Have we lost our pilot?"

even then, we can trust our lives to God! *Even then*, we can say, "Father, my times are in Your hands." We can know it, and we can stand on it! Even poor Job, sitting amongst the ashes and complaining bitterly—even Job was still in God's hands!

I don't understand all the whys surrounding Job. I don't understand all the whys of anyone's sufferings.

> Why does a little boy die of leukemia?
>
> Why does a young father die of a sudden heart attack?
>
> Why does a mother with three little children die in an automobile accident?
>
> Why is a defenseless seven-year-old sexually molested by her stepfather?
>
> Why does a saintly grandmother die an excruciatingly painful death?

You don't know how much I would love to avoid these questions! It would be so much safer to stick with the easy ones like, "Why does it hurt when I fall off my bicycle?" But if we are to face the subject of hurts honestly, even the impossible questions have to be dealt with. You are living them. You are asking them. And you need a response. The following responses are fairly obvious.

Satan is the ruler of this earth. As long as we live on this earth we are subject to his attacks. (There will be more about that in the next chapter.) God did not promise us a life of no problems. In fact, He said the very opposite: "Many are the afflictions of the righteous" (Psalm 34:19 KJV).

Okay, we made it through those. Now, what about some answers to the *impossible* questions? That is not so simple.

I *want* to say, "That should never have happened, not to you or to your loved one."

I *can* say, "I'm sorry."

I *can* say, "I feel for you. I'm with you. I'm praying for you."

But can I tell you why that unthinkable, that "un-world experience," as Joyce Heatherly puts it, has happened?

No, I can't. Decisions made in heaven are not often understandable to us. Job's friend, Elihu, gives wise counsel to Job when he asks, "Why should you fight against him (God) just because he does not give account to you of what he does?"

Lauren Stratford's interpretation of Elihu's counsel is that it is useless to struggle with the whys when God chooses not to answer. Why? Because His ways are not our ways. We will not always understand His ways, even when His ways seem wrong to us, and they appear to be one colossal mistake. I can make one statement that is absolute truth.

God's ways are always perfect!

Though we may never understand the whys of our sufferings until we get to our eternal destination, I encourage you with the assurance that God's faithfulness will be unto you even as it was with Job. I can equally encourage you with the promise that God will deliver you from your suffering just as He rescued Job. Whether it be through human means, through divine intervention or through the ultimate means of passing into life eternal:

God will deliver you!

The purpose of our lives does not lie in how we made our days upon this earth more pleasurable. The only thing that really counts is how we have chosen to prepare our lives for eternity.

That is not a cop-out. That is the pure, biblical truth. If I have lived a life of ease, with nary an encounter with pain, and yet I meet my Maker unprepared, my life will be worthless. On the other hand, though my earthly life be tried and tested as if by fire, and I go from suffering to suffering, if it drives me to an intimate relationship with God, my life could not be richer.

Life on this earth must only be measured by eternity's values.

> So we do not look at what we can see right now, the troubles all around us, but we look forward to the joys in heaven which we have not yet seen. The troubles will soon be over but the joys to come will last forever (2 Corinthians 4:18 TLB).

Have you ever felt that God was asking you to be a Job? Have you had to walk in Job's shoes? Was your first and last reaction, "Please God. Not me!"

Then let me share the ending to Job's story—not his demise, but his triumph:

Job was healed.

7 sons lost were replaced with 7 more sons.

3 daughters lost were replaced with 3 more daughters.

7,000 sheep lost were replaced with 14,000 sheep.

3,000 camels lost were doubled to 6,000.

500 teams of oxen lost became doubled to 1,000.

500 donkeys lost became doubled to 1,000.

And in all the land there were no other girls as lovely as the daughters of Job. . . . Job lived 140 years after that, living to see his grand-children and great-grandchildren too. Then at last he died, an old, old man, after living a long, good life (Job 42:15-17 TLB).

Just as Job went through the fire, so may we—you and I. Job believed. Job broke. Job was restored. Job was rewarded.

If we are called to be Jobs, we can be confident that God will still be the God of our lives. To know that "He doeth all things well" is enough for me. I can be confi-dent in His direction.

So can you!

When Trouble Comes, Where Are You?

♦

The enemy is approaching. I hear the faint sounds of battle, but they are way off in the distance. No need to fear. No need to worry—not yet.

I've got plenty of time!

The monotonous drone of military tanks is getting louder. But they're still far off.

I've got time!

Flares light up the sky, but only on the horizon.

There's still time!

The sounds of rockets split the air. But the sounds are still far away.

No need to worry!

Jet engines are screaming above. But I can't see them yet. The drone of the tanks, flares bursting light in the sky, rockets exploding. They are all getting closer... closer... closer.

I know they will get here, sooner or later. But I still have plenty of time to prepare.

No need to panic!

Do I have news for this would-be warrior! He is as good as dead! He is not even in the battle yet, and can already be assured of casualty status!

What soldier lies down on open ground, with his rifle and helmet beside him, and goes to sleep, knowing the enemy is fast approaching with a full armament of artillery? He might as well hang a sign around his neck that reads, "Here I am. Come and get me." He is inviting his own defeat and handing one more victory to the enemy—free of charge!

"I'm not that foolish!"

Oh, really? Maybe *you* aren't, but I've been that foolish many times. I have also known other men and women who have cried, after the fact, "How stupid of me! How could I have been so foolish?"

By now every one of us should know that we are living on a battlefield. The enemy has shot at us, kicked us, knocked us down, trampled on us and has even tried to bury us. The enemy has lied to our faces. He has gossiped about us. He has stabbed us in the back. He has turned our friends and even loved ones against us.

Sadly, most of us are unprepared for the battles we encounter. We are standing on the front lines yet act as if we're in a demilitarized zone! Well, believe me, Satan never calls, "Cease fire."

Good soldiers are well-prepared for battle. They learn, *before* the enemy strikes, how to defend themselves. Their training in boot camp prepares them for every conceivable method the enemy might use against them. They stay in shape physically, and they stay alert mentally so that when the enemy does strike, they will be in top form, ready for any eventuality. I have never heard of a surviving soldier who has gone into the heat of battle only to remain passive and noncombative!

So why is it, then, that in our spiritual battles, Christians often believe that:

1. Satan is not a threat to Christians.

2. If we ignore him, he'll go away.

3. If we even mention his name, we are giving undue glory to him.

4. Learning his tactics is a waste of time.

If these premises are true, why does the Word of God exhort us to resist the devil and to be careful to not give him a foothold in our lives? Why does the Bible warn us that Satan is prowling around on this earth just looking for people to destroy? If the enemy were not a danger, why would Scripture entreat us to arm ourselves for battle?

> Put on God's whole armor [the armor which God supplies to the soldier], that you may be able successfully to stand up against [all] the strategies and the deceits of the devil (Ephesians 6:11 AMP).

Believe me, armor is not worn to make a fashion statement! The Christian's armor is not worn for looks, for decoration or for comfort. It is worn to protect him against a very real and present danger to his soul. We may lose every material possession we own, and still come out winners. But the person who loses his soul loses his life! It cannot be gained back.

I received a letter from a victim of Satan's fiery darts. She had never learned that he was a danger to her. So when the enemy came in and mowed her down like dry tinder, she didn't know what had hit her.

It took several months for her to get back on her feet emotionally. She decided that she needed to become stronger spiritually. So she went to a Christian bookstore and bought several books on spiritual warfare. She was so encouraged after studying how to fight Satan that she took them to church and showed them to her pastor. His reaction stunned her.

"We don't need to learn about the enemy, dear. We only need to know the love of Jesus." Her pastor politely suggested that she get rid of her newly-acquired books and stick with the Bible. She went home crestfallen and confused.

I could hear her confusion as she wrote to me. "What did I do wrong, Lauren? I know that Satan has had me under his thumb for years now. I've been up and down more times than a horse on a merry-go-round!"

I think her next statement was the most crucial and "right-on" of all. She wrote, "I know I'm in spiritual warfare with Satan. But I didn't know how to fight him until I began to study those books and the Bible verses that they referred me to. Believe me, the next time the enemy attacks, I'll know what to do. I'm prepared!"

Amen to that! The hurting person is critically vulnerable to the attacks of the enemy. Satan does not have the manners of a gentleman! When he sees a person whose heart has been wounded, he wastes no time. He moves right in for the kill!

"It's Just Life"...or Is It?

Certainly some problems are simply a part of living. They happen because we are human beings who are living in a troubled world. In order to fight the battle properly, we must be able to differentiate between those problems which are "just ordinary problems," and those which indicate we are really under the deliberate and calculated attack of Satan.

Everybody knows about the kind of days when...

> The kids wake everyone in the house up at 5 A.M.
>
> The toast burns and the eggs scorch.
>
> Someone knocks the orange juice over and ruins the newspaper.
>
> The school bus honks before the kids' lunches are made.

The car battery is dead...the car keys are lost.

And on and on and on....

We can all count on having those kind of experiences once in awhile. They require an extra measure of the grace of God to prevent our screaming bloody murder. And, with His help, we usually make it through.

But what if *every* day becomes like that? What if our weeks seem to go from bad to worse? What if we begin dreading the thought of getting up in the morning, and by day's end we seem incapable of functioning? That is when, I believe, Satan has stepped into the "normal" problems and has taken over.

It is vitally important to know what signs and symptoms indicate this kind of assault. And it is equally important to know which problems have come from Satan, and necessitate our immediate spiritual action and authority.

Consider these possibilities.

1. Have "that's just life" problems become repetitive and worsened until they seem like a pattern, and not just typical daily frustrations?

2. Have those problems begun to affect the functioning of other family members?

3. Are they spilling over into other areas of daily living?

4. Are you beginning to fear that everything that happens is going to be bad?

When Satan steps into the picture and begins to take over, our situation is no longer "ordinary." Not only must the problems be handled, but the enemy must be confronted.

There are some problems that come directly from the enemy's camp at the outset. For example:

+ Fear that controls us.

+ Guilt that overwhelms us and keeps us burdened down.

+ Depression that deepens daily or hits us frequently and leaves us dysfunctional.

+ Avoidance of Christian fellowship because we either feel we won't fit in, or think others are better Christians than we are.

Other problems may arise from past or present occultic participation, such as:

Feeling continually and hopelessly drawn back to those practices.

Feeling overpowered by Satan even though we have confessed those practices and have given our lives to Jesus.

A compulsion to harm ourselves physically, by cutting, burning or even suicide.

Any of these situations most assuredly indicate that Satan has become either the *controller* of an ordinary problem, or the *organizer* of a calculated scheme to defeat us. In these cases, we must put on the armor of God, as listed in Ephesians 6:14-17. We must "... resist and stand your ground on the evil day [of danger], and, having done all [the crisis demands] to stand [firmly in your place]" (Ephesians 6:13 AMP).

The Word of God promises that, having done so, we

will "...be [empowered through our union with Him]" and that we will be able to "draw our strength from Him [that strength which His boundless might provides]" (Ephesians 6:10 AMP).

This is *our privilege, our right*, and *our inheritance* as children of God.

Are You an Easy Prey?

But what if we go into battle unprepared? It is difficult to retreat from spiritual conflict. To put it bluntly, once you're there, you're there! You cannot prepare for a crisis after the crisis has begun. The word "prepare" means to get ready for a specific purpose *beforehand*— not during or after.

Preparation must take place *before* we are nose to nose with our enemy. How many of us have gone through a period, maybe for several months or for a few of the more fortunate ones, perhaps even for several years, in relative good fortunes. No really trying times, no distresses that press us up against a wall, no serious family problems. We may have felt virtually unreachable and untouchable by the enemy.

What is the normal pattern of our spiritual life when things are going pretty well? It's not surprising to find that our daily Bible reading and prayer time decrease. It is often typical for our church attendance to become sporadic. Our thought life tends to become less centered on things above, along with our affections. To sum it up, we have become so accustomed to the good life that our need for Jesus isn't quite as intense as it was during that last trial.

The fact is, it's a *Big Mistake* to get used to the good times and to forget what we learned when things were not going so well.

A *Big Mistake* to think our trials are far behind us now, and there are nothing but good times ahead.

A *Big Mistake* to let our spiritual nurturing fall by the wayside during the good times.

A *Big Mistake* to stand unprepared, naked, and unaware before the enemy who can destroy our soul.

"Oh, but he's gone. He doesn't bother me anymore. I leave him alone, and he leaves me alone," we declare confidently, and sometimes with pride.

Do you know what I think of that kind of reasoning? It reminds me of a person who jumps out of the airplane without first checking out his parachute. His reasoning? "It's always worked before. I don't have to keep going through all of those boring checks every time. It's cool now!"

Yes, and "cool" it might seem until the body hurtles through the air at breakneck speed and comes to a sickening halt, slamming into the earth. Parachutists go through a rigorous set of checks before every jump. They know the utter folly of climbing into that airplane unprepared.

Please allow me to categorize that kind of thinking in my own terminology. "It's just plain stupid! You are asking for it. And if you crash, someone less polite might be tempted to say, 'I told you so'!"

We should never forget that, as Edith Schaeffer so aptly puts it, "Persecution and affliction are a normal part of the Christian life."[1] It is neither unusual nor rare. It is normal. It will happen—sooner or later! You and I are no more exempt from the hurts of this earthly life than we are exempt from the IRS! Just as sure as we pay taxes, we will also pay our dues as members of the human race.

When Trouble Comes...

Where are you? Does trouble find you far from God, basking in the "security" of your own good times? When trouble comes, do you feel like you are so far from God that you have to start all over with Him? When trouble comes, do you scream in panic, "God, where are You? Can You hear me?"

There is a verse in the Book of Psalms that has been a guideline and inspiration to me for many years. As usual, David is talking about his troubles. But he is also sharing what he has learned to do before his troubles come.

> The one thing I want from God, the thing I seek most of all, is the privilege of meditating in his Temple, living in his presence every day of my life, delighting in his incomparable perfections and glory.
> *There I'll be when troubles come.* He will hide me. He will set me on a high rock out of reach of all my enemies. Then I will bring him sacrifices and sing His praise with much joy.
> Listen to my pleading, Lord! Be merciful and send the help I need (Psalm 27:4-7 TLB, italics mine).

David may have had his ups and downs, but he was no dummy! He gives us three of the most vital conditions for the hurting person's survival.

1. David says that he lives in the Lord's presence every day of his life.

2. He confirms that he'll be there "when troubles come."

3. Because he has never strayed from the Lord's presence; because he is already there when troubles come, he has the assurance (without panic) that he will receive from the Lord the help he needs.

Friends, I cannot think of a more sensible, a more workable, or more dependable plan for the Christian to follow. As sure as one plus one equals two, these three steps equal sure survival for the hurting person.

We must learn to live as close to the Lord as we can, every day of our lives, so when trouble does come, we will already be in the presence of the Lord. We will say as David said, "There I'll be when troubles come"—in His presence, safe and secure, already protected from the enemy.

In doing this, we needn't drop everything in panic and freeze in fear, crying out, "God, I'm so far away from You, but I need You now!" I don't have to fall to my knees and spend hours in desperate prayer trying to gain back the relationship with the Lord I should have been having with Him all along.

Why? Because *I have been walking with Him every day.* During the good times and during the bad times. I have been meditating on His Word. I have been talking to Him daily, consciously nurturing the most important friendship in my life. I have kept myself prepared, so that when the enemy attacks, I am covered!

When the old predator, Satan, sees that I am prayed up, read up, armored up and walking hand in hand with Jesus, his little red flags are going to shoot up, "Warning. This person is prepared for battle. *Not an easy prey!*"

Help!

Yes, the attack will come—it is inevitable. And help is on the way, but only if you call for it. It is better, for sure, if you've been living close to the Lord every day. It is better, for sure, if you have been supplying yourself with spiritual food. It is better, for sure, if you have never removed the armor of the Lord. Each of these becomes a bonus to you when you find yourself in the heat of the battle.

But if you haven't prepared yourself, don't give up. Jesus never abandons us. No matter where we are or what condition we are in, help is always available. Psalm 56:9 couldn't be more encouraging:

> The very day I call for help, the tide of battle turns. My enemies flee! This one thing I know: God is for me! (TLB).

Even if you have wandered far off in your walk with the Lord, He will still be attentive to your cry. When David writes, "The very day I call for help, the tide of battle turns," he doesn't put a string of stipulations ahead of it requiring us to meet each of them before we can call for help. The fact is: The Lord hears *all* who are in need and cry out to Him, and He never fails to answer. The second we cry out to Him, the answer is dispatched.

Cry out the minute you find yourself in trouble! So many hurting souls have confided in me that they have found themselves in battle insufficiently prepared. When the conflict exploded around them, they felt guilty about the weakness of their spiritual condition. They didn't feel they had the right to call on the Lord when things got tough.

I have seen the toll of the lonely battle etched upon their faces. The human spirit, however valiant, is no match for the supernatural powers of darkness. Jesus never intended that we fight the enemy in our human strength. In doing so, we are destined for failure.

Paul recognized that he was no match for the enemy. He swallowed his pride and said it boldly:

> I think you ought to know, dear brothers, about the hard time we went through in Asia. We were really crushed and overwhelmed, and feared we would never live through it. We felt we were doomed to die and saw how powerless

we were to help ourselves; but that was good,
for then we put everything into the hands of
God, who alone could save us... (2 Corinthians 1:8,9 TLB).

There is no time for feeling guilty, ashamed, or sorry
about yesterday, when you need God's deliverance today!
You don't have time to stand around brooding over what
might have been or what *should have been*. That's exactly what the enemy of your soul wants you to do! You
cannot afford any ill-spent time. Whatever your mistakes or sins were, ask God's forgiveness, and raise your
head up and cry,

> *"Help, Lord!"*

Don't stand there, and let Satan beat on you. He will
whip you to a bloody pulp if you let him. Don't give him
permission. You are not his whipping post!

Do you know who you are in Christ Jesus?

> Do you not know that your body is a temple
> of the Holy Spirit, who is in you, whom you
> have received from God? (1 Corinthians 6:19
> NIV).

> Don't you know that you yourselves are
> God's temple and that God's Spirit lives in
> you? (1 Corinthians 3:16 NIV).

Your safety lies in the God who dwells in your heart.
God within you is your warrior and "greater is He that is
in you, than he that is in the world" (1 John 4:4 KJV).

He will do battle for you.

" 'Lord,' I pled, 'you are my only place of refuge. Only
you can keep me safe' " (Psalm 142:5 TLB).

When we fear for our lives, we have forgotten in whom

our safety lies. We have forgotten who our real protection is. Where will you be when trouble comes? Will you know that your body is the temple of God? Will you know that you have all of God within you? Will you be looking to your earthly temple made of clay, or will you be looking to the temple of your spirit where God dwells?

You can be sure that God will hear your cry.

You can be equally as sure that your earthly body will cry back, "Oh, no! Not again! I'm no match for Satan. I don't want to get beaten up anymore!" That heartfelt cry reflects the very condition some of us are in. Bruised. Bloodied. Torn apart. And defeated.

If we will only dwell in the Lord and let Him dwell in us every day of our lives, during the good times as well as the bad times, we can be safe. Marie Chapian writes words that Jesus Christ surely says to us:

> No matter *where you are*, and no matter *what is going on around you*, you are safe in Me. I am your refuge and dwelling place. My arms never tire of holding you.[2]

It's essential to realize "the eternal God is your refuge and dwelling place" (Deuteronomy 33:27 AMP). If you will but dwell in Him at all times, you will find that:

> Yes, he alone is my Rock, my rescuer, defense and fortress—why then should I be tense with fear when troubles come?
> My protection and success come from God alone. He is my refuge, a Rock where no enemy can reach me (Psalm 62:6,7 TLB).

I know the fear of being hurt again and again, and I have heard others say, "I've been hurt so often that I know it's bound to happen again. I'm just unlucky. Maybe God has it in for me."

Oh no, dear one! God doesn't have it in for you. *Satan does!*

God is not prowling around the earth to find those who are ripe for devouring. Satan is!

Jesus says to you, "For I know the plans I have for you.... They are plans for good and not for evil, to give you a future and a hope" (Jeremiah 29:11 TLB).

What a disservice it would be for me to promise you that you will never hurt again. It needs to be restated that as long as we are leaving footprints on this earth, we are going to suffer the afflictions and trials of this all-too-human life!

I received a card from a young man who wrote:

> Thank you for telling how it really is. I've been a Christian nearly all my life, and all I've heard preached is that the Christian's life is always wonderful.
>
> Well, my parents were tragically killed in an auto wreck. It's taken me a long time to get over it. What I'm getting at is when everyone tells you it's always a bed of roses, but never tells how life can hurt sometimes—even though I kept reading the Bible and praying after my parents were killed—I knew inside that I blamed God and hated Him.
>
> Thank you, Ms. Stratford, for confirming to me that life isn't always a bed of roses, even for the Christian.

Since this young man didn't include a street address along with the city and state he lives in, I couldn't answer his letter personally. Instead, I will answer him along with those of you who feel the same way he does.

Dear Friend,

I admire your courage for telling me how

you're really feeling. Thank you for sharing a heart full of hurts. Your determination to hang in there when the odds were against you is an inspiration to me!

You are not any less a Christian or any less loved by the Lord Jesus because of the tragedies in your life. He weeps with you and longs to carry you in the shelter of His arms. When life isn't a bed of roses and troubles come your way, you'll be safe in Him.

Sharing the love of Jesus,

Lauren

Where will *you* be when troubles come? David had the right answer.

> I shall live forever in your tabernacle; oh, to be safe beneath the shelter of your wings! (Psalm 61:4 TLB).

Will you answer with David, "There I'll be when troubles come"?

It's the only safe place to be.

12

God Wastes Nothing— Even This!

✦

"Sammye, your house is on fire!" the woman was yelling at the top of her voice as she ran into the beauty shop. Sammye didn't look up. Sitting under a hair dryer, she was engrossed in a woman's magazine.

"Sammye! Sammye! Your house is on fire!" The woman yelled frantically. Again, no response.

The beautician ran over to the dryer and pulled the hood up. Sammye looked up from her magazine. "Hi, Barb. How did you know I was here?" she asked. Then she saw the look on Barb's face. "What's wrong?"

Before she could get the words out, Barb repeated it for the third time. "Sammye, your house is on fire! Hurry! I'll drive you home." With rollers still in place, not even taking the time to lay the magazine down, Sammye ran out of the beauty shop with her friend.

Barb drove through red lights, her tires squealing as she cut corners too fast for safety. Sammye had the car door open before Barb could pull up to the curb. She tumbled out and dashed across the street, jumping over fire hoses as she ran. Barb was close behind.

Several of Sammye's neighbors had already gathered around to comfort her. Sammye stood motionless with her hands on her face just staring at her house which by now was engulfed in flames.

One of the neighbors took Barb aside saying, "She's

184 ✦ Lauren Stratford

in shock, Barb. You'd better stick close to her, because she's going to fall apart at any moment. She's really going to need you."

Barb walked over to Sammye and put her arm around her. "Sammye, I'm here. We'll get through this together." Sammye showed no indication that she had even heard Barb's words. She just stood there watching her house burning to the ground. Barb tightened her grip around Sammye's waist expecting her to slump to the ground at any moment.

"I've lost everything, Barb," Sammye whispered. "By this evening, it'll be nothing but smoldering ashes."

Her voice began to break as she thought of some of the irreplaceable memoirs. Photos of loved ones. Cherished love letters. Pink baby booties she had bought the day she learned she was pregnant. The booties had never been used—she had suffered a miscarriage.

"I've lost it all. Everything, Barb. Everything! The furniture and clothes can be replaced, but the things that mean the most to me are gone forever."

Turning away from the fire, she tried to collect her thoughts. Then she amazed Barb as she continued. "But you know, Barb, I've learned something about God in the midst of all my losses in life. I've learned enough to know that if He allows even all of this to be taken away, He's going to replace it with something else. Maybe something even better! Somehow He's going to turn even this loss into a gain. God will not let this be for nothing."

Barb didn't say it out loud, but she thought to herself, *Sure, Sammye. Sure.*

Sammye read the look on Barb's face. "Barb, I know what you're thinking." Seeing the disbelief that was still etched on Barb's face, she added, "I don't know how, but God's wastes nothing, not even this. Be patient, Barb. You'll see!"

Even This!

I would have to agree—Sammye was right. Jesus can take the "uglies" in our lives and transform them into things that not only glorify Him, but can also be used for our good. No, I don't know *how*. I only know that He can and He *does* do it when we allow Him to.

As we turn to Jesus in the midst of our most unwanted circumstances, just as Sammye did, He will never allow that trial to be wasted! There is nothing in our lives that God will allow to be meaningless once we ask Him to step into the picture.

I realize that statement is bold and all-encompassing. I know it cries out to be questioned.

"Even the time my husband raped me when he was drunk?"

Yes, even then.

"Even the time my best friend grew jealous of my success and lied about me to other people?"

Yes, even then.

"Even the time my little son watched as his puppy was run over by a teenager who was just out looking for kicks?"

Yes, even then.

"Even the time my husband had a heart attack after losing a job promotion?"

Yes, even then.

"Even the time my husband and I had to sign our teenage daughter into a rehabilitation hospital when we found out she was addicted to drugs?"

Yes, even then.

"Even the time I had to watch my precious wife die an agonizing death with cancer? She was only 28 years old, you know. And she left three little children behind. You mean, even then?"

Yes, even then.

Even the "uglies"?
Even the "unfairs"?
Even the "not possibles"?
Even the "unthinkables"?
Yes, yes! *None are wasted!*

"Right, Lauren, it must be easy for you to sit at your desk and write those words," you cry from a broken heart. "They're just words to you. They're the *real thing* to me!"

I wish you knew my feelings as I sit and write. My carnal nature doesn't want to write, *Even this.* I want to cry out with you, "It's not fair!" My human mind can't comprehend the "even this?" kind of trial.

But my spirit says something quite different. That's because my spirit communes with the heart of God.

My spirit knows that even in the very worst of my own trials, in the most horrible of situations, God has ultimately taken *a waste* and made *a something* out of it. Someone was blessed. Someone was made stronger. Someone gave his life to Jesus. Someone finally put his all into the hands of the Lord. Someone else was encouraged by my courage, and on and on.

Let Satan do his foulest deed. Let the old bully take his best shot. He cannot overpower the supernatural touch of Jesus Christ once Jesus steps into the situation. *Satan is no match for God—never was, isn't now and never will be!* No matter what Satan does, God is committed to changing the worst into something for our best.

> And we know that all that happens to us is working for our good if we love God and are fitting into his plans (Romans 8:28 TLB).

Here we are at that "all things" and "even this" and "surely not that" way of thinking again. But that is

God's Word. "All that happens is working for our good." All that Satan can do is but clay in the Master Potter's hands.

Whatever our Father allows to touch our lives or the lives of those we love, no matter how ill-suited it seems, ultimately works for our spiritual good. And there is nothing more vital than that which affects our spiritual life.

There are certainly two ways my own life's afflictions might be viewed.

Some people have written or said to me: "I've always had a lot of questions concerning human suffering. I've had so much suffering in my life, and I've become bitter about it. But as I look at your life and what God has made out of your personal nightmare, I see that He really can take my suffering and turn it into something for good."

Others may only have heard of the horrors. They might have missed the message of my miraculous deliverance, and the way God has used me to encourage other victims to have courage, to speak up and to seek help. These would surely say, "What a waste! All those years for nothing! Satan sure got the glory there!"

That is why I tell my story. That is why I bare the ugliest of the ugly. If God can transform the worst Satan can devise into encouragement for the hurting, the frightened, the depressed and even the suicidal, then *absolutely nothing* has been wasted in my life! Not one act of sexual abuse. Not one photo of kiddie porn. Not one episode of ritualistic abuse. Not one child whose life was snuffed out. Not one minute, one hour, one day or one year was wasted! Satan's worst has been no match for the loving and healing touch of Jesus Christ.

Satan meant it for evil. God used it for good. Satan wanted to waste me. God wants to use me.

Yes, I'll pay the price. *Will you?*

Yes, I'll allow God to take the waste and change it into encouragement for another sufferer. *Will you?*

Yes, I'll reveal the ugliness in my past in order that another who is hiding something will have the courage to uncover it. *Will you?*

The "Sally Jessy Raphael Show"

I was on the "Sally Jessy Raphael Show" last year. I had been told that one of the other guests was Paul Valentine, the high priest of "The Worldwide Church of Satanic Liberation." His appeal seems to be mainly to teenagers and college-age young people. Knowing nothing about him, another guest who was a probation officer and an authority on satanism showed me a video of Paul giving the oath of allegiance to satanism to a teenage boy. Paul was informing the boy that he might be shunned by family and friends and that he might have to give up relationships he had held dear.

He looked into the boy's eyes and asked him, "Are you willing to do that?" The boy said in as solemn and sincere and dedicated a voice as I have ever heard, "Yes, I am."

That, and other satanic activities were vividly portrayed in the video. They upset me so much that I didn't want to be on the program with Paul. To top it off, I was given a copy of a multipage application form that prospective members of Valentine's group had to read, fill out and sign. After somehow managing to wade through it, I was adamant. *I was not going on the program! And that was that!* No way was I going to spill out my most horrendously painful memories to a satanist! My only other thought was, "Thank God he hasn't read my book!"

Because of some of the things I had seen on the video, I went to bed that night feeling dirty and abused all over again. My heart was heavy with sorrow, and my spirit was deeply troubled. I tossed and turned all night thinking about the teenagers who were getting involved in satanism. All I knew to do was pray. I tried, but I couldn't. There was just no way to tell God what I was feeling. But of one thing I was certain—God knew I didn't want to be on that program, and He surely wasn't going to require me to fulfill my obligation!

However... a funny thing happened on the way to the "Sally Jessy Raphael Show." While riding in the limousine, God began to work on my heart. If He had spoken in an audible voice, I could easily have put my hands over my ears and blocked out His voice. But when God speaks in that still, small voice to the inward heart, there's no way of not hearing Him. I had no choice but to sit there and pay attention.

So I listened, and I heard what I did not want to hear. That's right! He wanted me to go on the show!

My only response to Him, which I repeated over and over again was, "But God, You don't understand. It'll be such a waste!"

It was obvious to me that I was listening to Him, but He wasn't listening to me! I only heard, "Go."

I have learned that I seldom, if ever, win an argument with anyone, much less with God. So I went!

Guess who I had to sit next to, I mean, *right* next to, so close we were almost touching? You're right. Paul Valentine. My first reaction was, "I don't believe this, God! If I have to do this, couldn't You have at least put another guest in between Paul and myself?" But again, God had a better idea!

To top this whole unwanted experience off, Paul's first words to me were, "The producers gave me your book to read last night."

I thought, "Oh, swell! The one thing I wanted the least was for this satanic high priest to read about the debasing and deplorable things other satanists did to me." I felt shamed and humiliated.

190 + ◆ Lauren Stratford

However . . . another funny thing happened. I kept my eyes glued to the floor, because I didn't want to look at this satanist sitting next to me. The Lord was not pleased! He began to work on my heart again. Or maybe I should say, He resumed the work He had begun during the ride to the studio.

Can you believe that a love for this Paul Valentine began to fill my heart? A sincere desire to tell him about the love of Jesus began to swell and spill over the edges of my soul. One thing is for sure—that love wasn't my doing! It could only have come from God. There was that still, small voice again. "Lauren, I died for Paul just as much as I died for you. I hung on the cross for him, too."

It hit me like an armored tank. My attitude changed 180 degrees. I had never been overwhelmed with such an urgency to show another person the love of God before.

The show began. The only opportunity to talk about Jesus was during the commercial breaks. I took advantage of every second to talk to Paul, telling him what Jesus had done for me and what He meant to me. My conversations with Paul were so obvious that one of the women in the audience stood up during the question and answer segment and asked me how I could stand to talk to "this man." I well recall her last sentence. "You even smiled at him!"

My response was not forced, nor was it insincere. "Ma'am," I said kindly, "I appreciate your concern. But I love this man with the love of Jesus Christ. I want him to see Jesus in me, and he never will if I hold hatred and anger in my heart toward him."

Two hours earlier, I would never have believed that I could have said that and meant it! But now, my one desire was for Paul to see the Jesus who died for him.

When the show ended, Paul wasted no time in turning to me. He looked at me intensely, with a searching look, and said just one sentence. But that one sentence is one I will never forget. It has kept me praying for him every day since.

"Lauren, I want you to know that I believe your Jesus has done something for you."

I was stunned! I wanted to leap up and yell, "Right on, Paul!" But I didn't. I kept my cool! As I turned to Paul, I felt my hand reaching out to him. I touched him briefly, just for a second or two, and said, "Paul, you're right. My Jesus *has* done something for me. But *my* Jesus can be *your* Jesus, and He'll do the same thing for you!"

Paul made no comment, but on the long ride from New Haven, Connecticut to La Guardia Airport in New York City, I thought over and over again, *A seed has been planted in Paul's heart. God, give it the increase and make it grow.*

Was pouring out my story worth it? You bet it was! Was my past of abuse and terror a waste now? No, a thousand times, no! God, in just one hour's time, took years of pain and shame and degradation and used them to speak to Paul's heart.

Perhaps he could not have been reached by anyone else's story.

God took my ugly hell and my question "Why God, why?" and wasted none of it! Every tear that was shed into my pillow in the darkness of night was saved. Every fear in my heart as I crouched in the corner on the floor was saved. Every agonizing moment as I made that long walk home from school, wondering what horror would be waiting for me behind the front door, was saved. Nothing, absolutely nothing, has been wasted!

Consider the nailing of Christ to the cross. What a shame! What a waste! A just man, an innocent man, put to death in the manner befitting a murderer. How tragic! Oh, but only in man's eyes.

God saw *beyond* the tragedy. He saw *beyond* the waste. He looked ahead to what He was going to produce. He saw the salvation of all mankind being brought forth from what you and I could only see as horror.

Joseph, the Man

Have you ever read the story of Joseph, the son of Jacob? Joseph was beloved by his father, more beloved than any of his eleven brothers. Those brothers were jealous of their father's special favor to Joseph, so they plotted to murder him.

Instead of killing the boy, however, at the last minute they sold him to a caravan of merchants for about eight ounces of silver.

Joseph's father had lovingly given his favorite son a coat of many colors. At the time he was sold, it was taken from Joseph and dipped into the blood of a slaughtered goat. Later, that blood-soaked coat was brought to his father, leading the poor man to believe that Joseph had been torn to pieces by a wild animal.

The caravan eventually delivered Joseph to Egypt, and there he was sold to Potiphar, an officer of Pharaoh. After a false accusation was made against him by Potiphar's wife, Joseph found himself in prison.

Joseph. What a waste!

That's our first impression. But the story doesn't end there. All of Joseph's difficulties were actually working for good!

Joseph, the Big Picture

Joseph, while imprisoned, was put in charge of two fellow prisoners, Pharaoh's chief butler and chief baker. With the help of the Holy Spirit, Joseph was able to successfully interpret their dreams. Soon he was called before Pharaoh himself. The Egyptian king wanted his dreams interpreted, too.

Joseph, again guided by God's Spirit, predicted seven

years of plenty and seven years of famine for Egypt and the surrounding countries. Pharaoh believed the prophecy, and appointed Joseph as a ruler over all the land of Egypt, assigned to store up food in preparation for the predicted seven-year drought.

He was given Pharaoh's ring to wear, clothed with fine linens, and given a gold chain to wear around his neck. Soon all Egyptians bowed their knees before him. Most important of all, God used Joseph to save countless lives in Egypt and all the nearby nations during the seven-year famine.

Joseph, the Bigger Picture

What a blessing! The apparent waste of Joseph's life was a blessing to millions of men and women, boys and girls. And it was Joseph himself who said the words that have become the very foundation and cornerstone for my life.

> You intended to harm me, but God intended it for good to accomplish what is now being done, the saving of many lives (Genesis 50:20 NIV).

All of the years. All of the sorrow. All of the unfairness. All of the plotting. All of the evil. All of the hurt. It has turned out to be for God's glory!

When Joseph's brothers came to Egypt to get grain for their family, they were suddenly face-to-face with Joseph, and they were understandably terrified. Joseph saw their fear and said to them:

> And now, do not be distressed and do not be angry with yourselves for selling me here, because it was to save lives that God sent me ahead of you. So then, it was not you who sent me here, but God (Genesis 45:5,8 NIV).

You see, while we are standing in the middle of our darkest hours, we see nothing but the pain and misery. God is, in the meantime, looking ahead to the bigger picture, anticipating what He's going to fashion out of our distress.

And He is not just doing it for His glory.

He is not just looking out for someone else's good.

He is working for our good, too!

From the Ashes

You and I are the wasteful ones. We have allowed our hurts to give birth to sins of the heart. Sins of the emotions. Sins of the spirit. We have chosen to harbor and nurture them until they control us.

Bitterness	Hatred
Grudges	Unforgiveness
Self-pity	Jealousy

The list goes on and on. These truly are a waste! We have allowed our hurts to waste our lives in sin.

And, at times, we may choose to sit amongst the ashes of our hurts, amongst the rubble of our unwanted circumstances. I speak from experience. There are some choices I wish I had never made. It is so tempting to stay in the "pits" and not even try to move. It is so tempting to say, "It's hopeless. It's no use. I might as well give up."

Sometimes the ugliness of our lives makes us feel useless, worthless and dirty. We are afraid to sift through the ashes of the past for fear of finding more debris staring us in the face. Well, it doesn't matter how full of ashes our lives are. The good news is that we are nothing more than sinners saved by God's grace anyway. None of us deserve God's goodness.

What *does* matter is that God uses the ashes of our lives, bringing forth beauty from them. If any of God's attention to my hurts was based on my perfection—past, present or future—I would be in deep, deep trouble. God's divine help depends only upon my *receiving* it.

All trouble changes us. We would have to be robots to not be affected by the trials of this life. And we aren't robots. We feel. We cry. We hurt.

The one thing we must ask ourselves is whether we will allow the enemy to change us for the worse or will we choose to allow the God of our salvation to change us for *His* best.

"How worthwhile are periods of our lives which seem to be a waste."[1] God will form our days to effect the kind of persons He wants us to be.[2]

I can assure you, dear one, *God will waste nothing in your life.*

– 13 –

I Give You My Comfort

◆

The speaker's first sentence was, "I want to tell you about my life. It's been so great!"

I've already heard enough, I thought to myself. *This is going to be a very long evening!* I sighed and settled back into my chair.

I have always hated to hear about somebody else's "great life." I usually get a little jealous, and once in awhile, a lot jealous. It's not that I wish they had had a *bad* life. Especially this person. Vicki is a good friend of mine, and I would never have wished her anything but the best. It was just that hearing about her life made me feel the hurt of my own childhood all the more. It reminded me of all the things I never had. And that was hard!

I felt my body begin to tense. If there had been a way of getting out of there without being noticed, I might have done so. But God, in His wisdom, had me sitting right where He wanted me—front row, middle table!

Vicki continued. "I was a hyperactive child. Never still. Into everything. And loving every minute of it. My mom and dad had a hard time keeping up with me, but they never showed me anything but love. I always knew they loved me."

I thought, *I don't believe this! Only thirty seconds have gone by, and she's already mentioned two of the most painful concepts I struggle with: the words "mom and dad" and "love."*

"Lord, may her speech be short," I prayed. I wasn't joking!

She continued. "I've had the most wonderful family." She spent at least five minutes describing them—her sister, a special aunt, grandparents, and the list went on . . . and on . . . and on. "I've had the neatest friends." Out came the list of her friends.

Is this ever going to end? My impatience was beginning to show. I couldn't get comfortable. Squirming in my chair, I crossed and uncrossed my legs about every minute-and-a-half. My impatience was not due to Vicki's talk being uninteresting. In fact, her choice of words and the enthusiasm that went with it were terrific.

She was not the problem. *I was!*

Vicki even used the phrase about living in "the house with the white picket fence"—the house I had dreamed and wished about for so many years. I couldn't keep from picturing her as a cute little girl running around with brightly-colored bows in her hair, picking daisies.

My heart began to ache, and I was beginning to fight back tears. I tried hard to keep my mind on what she was saying, but the usual questions demanded first place in my mind. They screamed louder and louder, finally drowning out her voice.

Occasionally, I heard her make comments about high school days and fun things she did in college. If my flesh and bones had their way, they would have stood up and said, "Enough is enough! I got the message twenty minutes ago." On the other hand, my spirit in Jesus Christ was saying, "You know, it's really neat that your friend has had such a loving and nurturing life. Be happy for her!"

Well, I was, really. I just couldn't help but think about the rest of us whose memories were somewhat less heartwarming.

Once Vicki finished I clapped. Everyone clapped. And I silently thanked God that the endurance test was over, and I had won. Not once had I tried to walk out of the room!

I was proud of myself. I even stayed to talk to several of the women, smiling and agreeing that Vicki's talk was interesting and inspiring.

Driving home, in Vicki's absence, I began to talk to myself out loud. "Vicki, I love you dearly. You're a good friend. But I will *never* be able to relate to your life, and you, for sure, will never be able to relate to mine."

There! I had spoken out what was bothering me the most. A dear friend of mine had lived a life that was so far removed from mine we were worlds, maybe even planets, apart!

No more than two months later, Vicki's world and mine met, or should I say, "collided." This same young woman, who had stood behind a podium, revealing the beautiful things in her life, was now sitting next to me on her sofa with her head on my shoulder, clinging to me for dear life.

I heard sobbing that could only have come from a broken heart. I heard groanings that poured out from a crushed spirit. I held a body that not only trembled, but shook deeply.

I guess I could say that I was shocked, but I wasn't. The first thing that came to mind was, *I should have known that no one has had a life with no trials, no pain and no struggles*.

What a privilege it was to show the love of Jesus to Vicki, to bind up the wounds of her heart with care and concern, and to say, "I know you're hurting. I've been there too."

She Hurts—She's Just Like Me!

It was a comforting experience. Not that she hurt, *but*

that she hurt like me! We had walked down some of the same roads after all. And though the *causes* of her pain were far different than mine, the *consequences* were identical.

No matter how much worse another person's trials may look to you, one statement bears repeating: Don't fall into the trap of comparing your pain with theirs. Pain is pain. When we hurt, we hurt. And whether your pain seems greater or lesser than mine, you need help as much as anyone else!

It didn't matter that my friend had different difficulties than I had. What mattered was that she was suffering. Her heart was breaking from hurts just as my heart had once been broken. In her brokenness, in her crushing, in her anguish and torment, we shared common ground.

The concept of common ground responds to the dilemma, "How in the world could my pain ever be used for good?" Without an answer, that question haunts us night and day. If I have asked it once, I have asked it a million times. My guess is that you have asked it more than once, too.

Common ground goes something like this:

You hurt.

I hurt.

You let me see *your* hurt.

I let you see *my* hurt.

Because *you* shared, I know you will understand me.

Because *I* shared, you know I will understand you.

The results?

Healing begins in both our hearts.

How could I point out the way to you if I had never been there myself? Would you follow my directions if you knew I had never traveled the road? No! In fact, you would more than likely not even bother to ask me.

Why did my friend Vicki risk exposing her wounds to me? Most people knew her as the "strong" Vicki, the "I've got it under control" Vicki, the role model for the successful and ever-victorious Christian. That's the way even I had known her.

Had something so terrible happened to her that her emotions couldn't handle the shock? Is that why she couldn't help but fall apart?

No way! Vicki had been accumulating hurts since a little girl. She was just as full of hurts as the rest of us. She also had buried them as deeply as some of us have. But one day, the Lord Jesus brought someone into her life who had also hurt—Lauren Stratford.

That's not so unusual. What was different was that I had just exposed the pain of my heart to the whole world through the book I had written. I had said, "My dear friend, here is my painful story."

Vicki had looked at my hurt and had felt a measure of my pain. Vicki was able to say, "Lauren hurts. She's just like me!" She realized that it was safe to expose her hurt to me.

The School of Hurting

I'll tell you, there is one school none of us would ever voluntarily attend! I would rather enroll in boot camp or swamp training than go through a course in hurting! The only problem is that very few of us, if any, pass through this life without having to go through The School of Hurting—whether we want to or not.

I'm a real bearer of good tidings, aren't I? You know, though, that it's the truth. As sour as it sounds, it really doesn't have to be. Nowhere does the Lord Jesus say that

unwanted circumstances such as suffering and affliction are for the purpose of making our lives miserable!
There's not one Scripture that even hints that the Lord
delights in the misery of His children. In fact, quite the
opposite is true.

Why then does He require that we go through The
School of Hurting? Some of those reasons have already
been shared.

1. Through our hurts, we can find an intimate
   relationship with Christ.

2. In our weakness Jesus becomes our strength.

3. The furnace of affliction molds and shapes
   us.

4. God will become our all in all, our sufficiency, everything we need Him to be.

The final reason that I share with you is the one that
for me, ties together everything else. It brings purpose
to a life of suffering. It not only makes the past bearable,
but it enables me to say, "I bless God for my pain."

No, I haven't gone off the deep end. (Not yet, anyway!)
The simple truth is that comfort and compassion are
only learned through our own hurting. The course is
basic.

1. I must know pain if I am to learn what pain
   feels like.

2. My experience with pain gives me compassion for another person in pain.

3. My compassion produces the gift of comfort
   which I can freely give away.

The word "compassion" means "to suffer with." It

means to enter into or join the suffering of another person; to become one with them in their pain.

The *suffering* Christ is also the *comforting* Christ. Who has suffered more than Christ? *No one!* Who else is spoken of as "the God of all comfort?" *No one!* Who else had more compassion for the infirm, the lonely, and the oppressed than Jesus Christ of Nazareth? *No one!*

How did Jesus expand His sense of compassion? Where did He get His ability to give such comfort that He truly is "The God of all comfort"?

Jesus literally became "a man of sorrows, and familiar with suffering" (Isaiah 53:3 NIV). "He took up our infirmities and carried our sorrows" (verse 4 NIV). Jesus grew in His compassion as He experienced humanity's suffering. He experienced it when His own heart was bruised and wounded as He hung upon the cross. He experienced it when He bore the sins of all mankind. No one has paid or ever will pay a higher price for compassion.

In His humanity, He made it through the school of suffering with an A+. His example is a hard act to follow, but we may all strive to learn from Him.

Putting Your Pain to Work

The Lord has taught me how to turn my pain around and make it work for me. I know that may sound a little strange, but if you will bear with me for a few minutes, I will show you that it really isn't.

Think of it this way. If I choose to remember my pain in bitterness, it will cripple me—permanently. But if I choose to put that pain to work for me, I will draw from my unwanted and uncomfortable experiences all that I need to comfort another person. That's what I chose to do with my pain—to turn it from an enemy into a friend.

Sometimes well-meaning "advisors" say to me, "The past is in the past. Why talk about it now? Just forget it!" When they add the sentence, "Why don't you just pretend like it never happened?" I sometimes think to myself, *They might as well be saying, "Why don't you just quit breathing?" It would be easier for me to quit breathing than to pretend my pain never happened!*

> For me, the past *did* happen.
> It *did* affect me.
> It *did* hurt.
> I cannot choose to ignore it.
> Or pretend it never happened.
> Or worse yet, forget it.
> But I *can* turn my pain around and use it to
>   comfort another person in pain.

That's the whole point of this book. We all agree that we are in pain and that we hurt. The issues are: "Now what do we do?"; "Can I make it hurt less or will it always hurt this bad?"; and "What am I to do with my pain?"

How well I can relate to these questions. My pain was drowning me. It was like a weight of stones, pulling me deeper and deeper into a sea of unbearable agony. I wore my hurts. They accompanied me every minute of the day. They slept with me at night. There was no escape.

At last I became so desperate that I literally begged Jesus to do something. Anything! Whatever! However! "God, You don't mean for me to drown in this pain forever! Do You?"

I personally think that God wants us to tell Him the way we really feel. I have found out that His shoulders are big enough to handle cries of desperation, no matter how they are voiced. When I became that desperate with myself and that honest with God, a strange thing began to happen. Traveling across the country to promote

Satan's Underground, I heard the same words of encouragement from almost every host. Program after program, interview after interview, the comments were identical.

"I'll have to admit, Lauren," the host would say, "that it wasn't easy getting through your book. After I would finish each chapter, I would think 'It can't get any worse.' Then I would read on and with each new chapter, it *did* get worse. I found myself asking God 'Why?' Why did she have to go through so much?"

I can't begin to count the times he or she would open a Bible to a particular passage of Scripture and say, "Lauren, this is just for you."

My heart would smile, because without sneaking a peek to see just where the host had turned in the Bible, I knew it was going to be 2 Corinthians, chapter one. With only one or two exceptions, the following verses would be read:

> What a wonderful God we have—he is the Father of our Lord Jesus Christ, the source of every mercy, and the one who so wonderfully comforts and strengthens us in our hardships and trials.
>
> And why does he do this? So that when others are troubled, needing our sympathy and encouragement, we can pass on to them this same help and comfort God has given us.
>
> You can be sure that the more we undergo sufferings for Christ, the more he will shower us with his comfort and encouragement.... But in our trouble God has comforted us—and this, too, to help you: to show you from our personal experience how God will tenderly comfort you when you undergo these same sufferings. He will give you the strength to endure (2 Corinthians 1:3-7 TLB).

The message was loud and clear. The Lord began to show me that I would be missing the whole point of my past if I didn't put my pain to work. I needed to pass on the comfort I had received, giving that same comfort to other people.

"I can do that, Lord. I long to comfort people in their pain. If my sufferings can be used to touch someone else's pain, then Lord, I give myself to You. Anoint my pain."

The first time I heard myself asking God to anoint my pain, I wasn't even sure why I had said it or what it meant. But the Lord knew. He said, *"My child, I want you to consecrate your pain for a higher purpose than for suffering. I will anoint your pain to be a comfort to the hearts of my other children who are still hurting."*

And so, "Anoint my pain, Lord," has been the unceasing prayer of my heart for the past year-and-a-half. As each day passes, I still feel an urgency to educate others about child pornography and sexual and ritualistic abuse, but the primary cry of my heart is that God would use me to bind up the wounds of the brokenhearted, to give them the same comfort with which I have been comforted.

Edith Schaeffer, the cofounder of the L'Abri community in Switzerland, writes: ". . . suffering or affliction or trouble of some kind needs to precede the giving or receiving of comfort."[1] We speak best of comfort when we speak from our own experience.

Moving On

It is a waste to remain in our hurts and never find anything in them but the pain, when a wealth of comfort for ourselves and for other people is available through our hurting.

We are *healed* by being comforted.

We are *blessed* by comforting others.

We must move on! Initially, it may be a discipline we simply have to choose to do. But as we grow in that discipline, it will become a blessing—for us as much as for those whose hearts to whom we have brought God's comfort.

I must stop and say something to you who are in a deep place of woundedness at this very moment. I speak it in all gentleness, with a heart full of love and compassion. There are "secondary gains" or side benefits from suffering. I can say this to you, because I have been a victim myself.

God only knows how much comfort means to a hurting person. Hurts shared are ever so much easier to bear. Comfort feels good! There is, however, a very real and present danger of settling into comfort, needing more and more and more.

I have learned the hard way that the more comfort I received, the more misery I could find that needed to be comforted. Please know that I speak for myself, and I'm not condemning anyone. I have simply been there, and in the middle of my pain, at times I have fallen into traps that Satan has set for me.

Pain blinds. Pain numbs. We can find ourselves almost helpless to move out of it. It is all-too-tempting to give in to it. I will tell you that as tempting as it is, there is an unequalled blessing for those who pray, "God, I give You my pain. Anoint it and use it to comfort someone else at their point of pain."

But I Still Hurt!

Yes, I know you're still hurting. Jesus knows you're hurting. And I'm still hurting in areas of my life, also. As God comforts me in my hurting, I will comfort you in yours. When I can say, "I feel your pain. May I share it with you?" you know I am for real. Let me encourage you that as you are willing to move on and comfort someone else, God will not abandon you in your own suffering. Whatever your suffering may still be, God will proportion His strength and grace so that you will be able to stand. *Just as we learned that His strength is equal to our weakness, so is His comfort equal to our affliction!*

You cannot outgive comfort. The more you show the compassion of the Lord Jesus to someone else, the more comfort He will give unto you. In my own life, I have not only found that His comfort was equal to my affliction, but it was greater.

> It's okay to hurt.
> It's okay to show your hurts.
> The Lord's comfort will equal your suffering.
> With the comfort you have received, comfort one another.

"Does that mean I have to *like* my pain?" No, not unless you are a whole lot different than me! I *can* say now, "I bless God for my pain." But not because I think it's so wonderful. I can say, "Bless God for it," because He has taken heart-wrenching anguish and transformed it, as only He can do, into something good.

"For to you has been given the privilege not only of trusting him but also of suffering for him" (Philippians 1:29 TLB). Do you know what my reaction used to be to the apostle Paul's words? I'd say, and usually out loud, "You've got to be kidding, right? The *privilege* of suffering? Come on, Paul! Tell me you're kidding." I wasn't trying to be facetious. It really did sound ridiculous to me. That is until I found out how God could snatch the suffering that Satan meant for my destruction and turn it into something good.

Matthew Henry, the biblical commentator, speaks of Paul as "the extraordinary sufferer."[2] How many of us have learned to honestly say along with Paul (in Philippians 4:11 KJV), "I have learned, in whatsoever state I am, therewith to be content"?

When I read that Paul was known as "the extraordinary sufferer," I said to myself, "There are a lot of things I would rather be known as besides that!" What an awesome title to have to earn! And yet, no one will ever know until we get to heaven just how many lives have been won to Christ and inspired and comforted because of the way Paul lived his life in the midst of continual hardships and severe afflictions.

Was Paul superhuman? No. He speaks perhaps more than anyone else in Scripture about being weak. How did this "weak" man then become known as "the *extraordinary* sufferer" and "the *great* sufferer"?

Paul allowed Christ to be his strength in his weakness and his comfort in his affliction. Even though he continued to go through numerous trials, *he chose to move on*, going in the strength and comfort of Christ, bringing that same strength and comfort to those about him.

No Greater Ministry

Edith Schaeffer summed up the whole of my thoughts when she wrote, "... He is not only preparing something *for* us, He is preparing *us* for something."[3]

You will never like the pain. *Pain hurts!* It's hard to cry tears of pain. It's hard to feel the ache in the pit of your stomach. It's hard to feel as if you have been bruised and bloodied by the blows of the enemy. It's hard when everything seems to be falling apart and you can't do anything about it.

It's hard, but it's okay!

God is allowing you to go through a process, a breaking, a melting, a shaping and ultimately, an anointing. Only through that process is He able to take hurt and suffering and transform it into ministry.

Have you been comforted in your pain? Have you felt the gentle squeeze of an arm around you from someone who said, "I know you're hurting, dear one. I feel your hurt. I share your hurt. I've been there too"? Do you remember how healing it was? Do you recall the warm feeling? If so, then you know the tender ministry of one who's been there before you. The road traveled alone is rough, but with a companion it is made smoother.

Do you bear the scars of battle? Have you been left wounded and bandaged, wounded again and rebandaged? I can tell you that those scars bear the proof of your suffering. If you will allow others to see them, they will not only bear testimony to your wounding, but testimony to your emerging a battle-scarred, but strengthened warrior.

Remember my friend Vicki? I don't want to leave her in this chapter sobbing on my shoulder, broken and longing for comfort. For perhaps an hour, Vicki grieved and began to open up the deeply-hidden wounds of her heart. Some of them went all the way back to her childhood. As she began to unburden her heart, the Lord brought forgotten wounds out into the open. She had buried them so carefully that only a work of the Holy Spirit could uncover them.

I put the very basics of comfort to work for her: Praying. Talking. Crying. Holding. Allowing her to be herself. Comforting her with the same comfort I had received. It works so beautifully! From that moment on, my friend has been a new Vicki!

She had shared with me months before that the deepest longing of her heart was to minister to those who suffer, and I knew there were hurting women in our church. I encouraged her to show the same transparency to those women that she had shown to me.

"If you will let them see you in your brokenness, the very thing you feared the most will draw them to you for ministry. They will say, 'She hurts. She's just like me!' When they come to you for counseling, you can comfort them with the same comfort you've received."

Vicki began to nod her head. "I know," she said quietly. "I know it's true."

"And Vic," I said, looking into her tearstained face, "God will bless and anoint your brokenness. Let it touch those women in their deepest points of pain."

Just a few days later, Vicki stood in front of our women's group and read a poem she had written the day before. It began with the sentence, "What is this brokenness I feel?" For the first time in her years of ministry to those women, she became the real Vicki. She read a poem about herself, the woman whose heart had been broken with "failures of the past, hurts in the present, and fears of the future." She read of tears, sweat, pain, anger, and frustration. It all came spilling out from behind crumbled walls that had just been torn down.

Was Vicki rejected? Did the women avoid her like the plague? Did they say to one another, "Good grief! Vicki's really messed up! She's falling apart. What's the matter with her anyway? She can't minister to us!"

Oh no! Far from it! Women came to her with their tears, their hurts, their bitter disappointments and every other kind of wound imaginable. Vicki was finally freed to move on. To make her pain work for her. To comfort the hurting with the comfort she herself had received.

I speak to you who are so bitter about the sufferings you're going through. Would you dare to pray the following simple prayer to the Lord Jesus?

> I give my pain to You.
> Take it.
> Use it.
> Anoint it.
> Amen.

– 14 –

Born from Affliction

◆

From the war grounds of Vietnam,
From the bottom of Chesapeake Bay,
From a Nazi death camp,
From a dark jungle in Ecuador.

Awesome testimonies of God's faithfulness have come from the most unlikely places and the most devastating circumstances.

Boom! The sound was deafening. A white phosphorous grenade exploded in the young sailor's hand. It was his own grenade—not the enemy's. Things like that aren't supposed to happen. Or are they?

Flesh burning and falling off by the pounds. Fingers blown away. An ear ripped off. Half of a human head mangled...torn...shredded. The sailor dives into the water, but his mutilated body keeps on burning. Flaming phosphorous can't be extinguished.

This man should be dead! And yet countless operations later, and after months in the hospital, one of America's most powerful ministers to teenagers begins his work.

Dave Roever—born from affliction!

Dave says, "Regardless of what you're going through, life is worth living!"

214 ✦ Lauren Stratford

Snap! The sound was not heard. The snap was not felt, but it was almost deadly. An exuberant and beautiful teenager, full of youthful life, dived into a lake, her sleek body cutting through the water effortlessly. Without warning, her head smashes against the bottom of the bay. Her spinal cord snaps, instantly paralyzing her from the shoulders down.

A teenager with dreams and promises for the future is sentenced to a wheelchair, dependent on others to care for even her most basic needs. She should have given up years ago. She didn't deserve this. And it wasn't fair! Yet this tragic accident gave birth to " Joni and Friends," a ministry that has inspired handicapped persons and educated the able-bodied.

Joni Eareckson Tada—born from affliction!

Joni says, "I'm able to smile, not *in spite of my circumstances,* but *because of my circumstances!*"

Sudden burning pain! Poisoned arrows and spears pierce the body of a strong young man. He slumps to the sandy shore of a river deep in the jungles of Ecuador, South America. Four other hale and hearty messengers of the love of Jesus Christ to the Auca Indians are felled by the same instruments of death.

What a blow to one of God's evangelistic powerhouses—foreign mission work. Or was it? Two of the widows, including Elisabeth Elliot, continued their efforts in the same jungle, showing the love of Jesus to the very Indians who had committed the murders. Five senseless deaths gave birth to a heretofore unmatched call to missionary outreach. Meanwhile, the oft-retold story challenged millions of hearts worldwide.

The undying inspiration of Jim Elliot, Nate Saint, Roger Youderian, Ed McCulley, and Pete Fleming— born from affliction!

Elisabeth Elliot, wife of the late Jim Elliot, has written,

"Through Jim's death, he spoke to more people than he could ever have through his life. Was it worth it? Unreservedly, yes! No question about it! Absolutely!"

Nazi war crimes! Mass murders in gas chambers. Human incinerators. Atrocities too unspeakable to mention. Over six million Jews slaughtered in the name of stamping out an "inferior" race. One particular woman found herself in the midst of those horrors at Ravensbruck, one of Adolf Hitler's infamous death camps.

Was this woman guilty of a crime? Did she deserve a sentence of death? Did her family members deserve to die by starvation and inhumane living conditions? No! They were a gentle and loving family who owned a humble repair shop for watches on a business street in Haarlem, Holland. During a purge in 1944, her family compassionately hid Jews in a small room on the top floor of their shop. They were discovered, arrested and herded like cattle to their appointed places of execution. This godly woman had to watch her dear sister, her father and thousands of other human beings die in the cruelest ways ever devised by one man. Oh, how full of hate she must have been! How bitter and vengeful and unforgiving she must have felt!

No, not quite.

This same woman spent the rest of her life teaching countless thousands of Christians how to forgive the unforgivable; how to turn life's most senseless evils into miracles of God's grace. This woman met up with one of her abusers several years after her release from the concentration camp and said, "I forgive you!"

Corrie ten Boom—born from affliction!

Corrie ten Boom said, "I was watching the actors during the filming of *The Hiding Place*.[1] The woman who came out of the prison gate looked tired and cold. Then I saw the woman who was playing Corrie ten

Boom. There I was, sitting and looking at my own story! Suddenly it was too much. I could not keep the tears back any longer. But through that a deep wound was healed. I knew why I had that time of suffering. I learned a lesson that I could share with many people the world over."[2]

Each of these individuals won a victory in battle, and each of these victories lives on even today. These triumphant men and women have proved the living reality of Psalm 118:14: "He is my strength and song in the heat of battle, and now he has given me the victory" (TLB).

Theirs would not be a story of victory—theirs would not even be a story—had it not been for the battle! "Oh yes," you say, "but if you talked with any one of them now, I'm sure they would have chosen to not have that unthinkable thing happen to them if they had had the choice!"

I'm not so sure about that. I wouldn't trade my "unthinkables." I have said that a thousand times over.

Besides, I have talked with Dave and with Joni's secretary. I have read the books of Corrie and Elisabeth. Every one of them has said, "It's been worth it. I thank God for my suffering. I see the miracle that God has wrought out of my tragedy. I am a more fulfilled person now than I ever could have been had I been spared my darkest hour."

When I look at these heroic men and women, I see "life abundant." I see determination forged in the heat of the furnace; I see understanding; and I see a consuming love of Jesus Christ that has come through intense suffering.

I see purpose.
I see courage.
I see winners.
I see single-minded commitment.
I see Jesus!

None of their afflictions stopped God's message. Instead, their afflictions were the cause and the means of God's message going forth. "Common" and "ordinary" men and women have been willing to allow God to use their afflictions for a greater good!

In the Midst of Your Affliction

And what about you? Are you "unusable" in the midst of your tribulations? No! You do not have to sit around and endure while you are going through that unthinkable trial. I'm reminded of the verse in Isaiah 40 that talks about mounting up with wings as eagles, running and not being weary and walking and not fainting.

Realistically, at my own low points I haven't always felt like running, or even walking! There are times when one cannot always soar like the eagle. There are times when one cannot always run on hind's feet. It may only be possible to crawl in the midst of your affliction. And that is sufficient!

We aren't all able to jump up and down and exclaim excitedly, "All right, Lord! Another trial!" Most of us feel completely cut asunder, struck by the enemy's arrows. But we can surely continue on in God's grace and in God's strength—even if we are crawling.

Did any one of those persons you just read about quit in the middle of their trial and say, "That's it, Lord. It's too much. I can't take any more! Stop the world. I want to get off"?

Yes! Dave Roever did. The unbearable pain of burned skin, of having dead tissue "debrided," literally scraped off his limbs, the skin grafts, the agony of trying to go through the physical therapy necessary to get his withered limbs to stretch—it was too much for any human being to bear. And in one of his darkest hours, Dave Roever pulled his IV tube out—on purpose!

Dave wanted to die. He wanted to check out. But as I

have heard him tell about it with humor in his voice, "I pulled out the wrong tube! Instead of pulling out the tube that was giving me the medications I needed to live, I pulled out the tube that fed me!"

Dave was in God's care even then! God saw ahead to a ministry He would give Dave, bearing in mind the thousands of high schoolers he would reach. God said, "Not yet, Dave. Not yet. I have plans for you."

If you can do nothing more than stay alive through your afflictions, it's all right. If you tell God you can't bear any more, that's all right too! God will understand, and He will put divine plans into action. He will not only sustain you, but He will *use* you in your severest affliction.

Yogi Berra, the great catcher for the New York Yankees and an inductee into the baseball Hall of Fame, made a comment that has become a trademark of his wit. He said, "It ain't over 'til it's over."[3] If I may take the liberty of paraphrasing that, I would say, "Even when *you* say it's over, it ain't over 'til *God* says it's over!" It will not be over until God's purpose for your life is accomplished.

And though your darkest hour seems chaotic, a total wreck, and nothing but a mess, through God's eyes, everything is going as He has allowed it. Everything is working for His good and for yours.

Until God says to you, "I've accomplished My will in your life; well done, thou good and faithful servant; it's time for you to come home"; *you have work to do*. You not only have something to do *after* your affliction, but you have work to do *within* your affliction.

I'm So Sorry God Can't Use You!

"It's a shame that you can no longer be used as a servant of God. What a waste to have to lie here when you could be out doing the will of God," she sighed.

I was greeted with those "sympathetic" words during one of my lengthy hospital stays. A well-meaning friend informed me that my time for serving Jesus was over. Wasn't that obvious since I was so ill, spending most of my time confined to a hospital bed?

Because I respected my friend as one who walked close to the Lord, I took her words to heart. I understood her to be saying that in the midst of another trial, a very long and severe trial, I could no longer be used by God. I went on to conclude that I was not even in God's will. How could sickness be God's will?

Oh, how my heart was crushed! I was hurting badly enough from my illness, both physically and emotionally. Now to be told that I couldn't be of any use to Jesus, whom I loved and wanted to serve with all my heart, was almost more than I could take. My spirits sank to new lows. How I grieved!

The doctors had given every indication that my illness was not only life-threatening but incurable. Now I wrestled with the final blow that, as long as I remained on this earth, I would never be used of God again! That was "defeat" spelled in capital letters to me!

Let me ask you something. Do you feel that you are "unusable" because you are going through a hard place in your life? Do you feel that something has gone very wrong because things aren't going just the way you planned them? They aren't quite like they are supposed to be? Let me encourage you that God can use you—*just as you are*. That He can use your difficulty—just as it is.

I can say that, dear one, because God used me when I was very ill and frightened. When I was dressed in nothing but one of those trendy hospital gowns. When I had a hairstyle that only a hospital pillow could arrange. When I was wearing the typical hospital jewelry of oxygen mask and IV needles and tubes with matching bruises and Band-Aids. Get the picture?

I can also say that God used my problem just as *it* was. Several near-death episodes with pain so severe that nothing would subdue it. An "orphan disease"[4] that required "orphan drugs"[5] that no pharmaceutical company wanted to manufacture. A prognosis so grim that my hospital social worker stood by me offering her emotional support as I filled out my last will and testament and made my funeral plans. Impossible? You bet! Unusable? Absolutely! But only through man's eyes.

I began to pray about my "unusability."

"God, why have You put me in this 'no man's land' where I can't serve You? Do I just have to lie here and vegetate?" I complained bitterly. And I questioned His wisdom. Oh how I questioned!

But from that moment on, I began to see my illness and my hospital stays from a totally different perspective. My normal modus operandi had always been to talk to my roommates about Jesus. The nurses and aides had all seen me clinging to my Bible quite literally for dear life. There was always a Bible verse on a piece of paper stuck on the wall. My favorite verse was, "I can do all things through Christ which strengtheneth me" (Philippians 4:13 KJV).

My sharing the love of Jesus was so automatic that I did it without thinking. It never occurred to me that God was using me. I had been blind to the fact that I was serving Him, even in *that* place!

While I was falling deeper and deeper into my "poor me" state of "I'm unusable now" attitude, friends who came to visit me began to make remarks like, "You know Lauren, I came here to encourage you, but I always leave feeling encouraged myself."

Then the nurses and aides began to tell me how inspired they were seeing how much my faith in the Lord Jesus helped me through the really bad times. They saw me trust Him through pain and tests, and endless blood drawing sessions—almost impossible episodes when it was time to find another IV site.

I noticed that the nurses began to put other patients right next to my wheelchair when I sat out in the hall for brief periods of time. Without a word spoken, I knew they were placing them there because they needed the same encouragement I had received from the Lord Jesus. Sometimes, I would even get them to laughing. Even if it was only for a minute or two, their spirits were lifted. And in return, my spirits were lifted, too.

Jesus began to make me aware of all of these people and what they were saying to me. I began to see that, no, I'm not unusable! The Lord Jesus is using me in my darkest hour, in the midst of my affliction, just the way I am. He put it all together and used it for good! Wow! When I began to see what God was doing, I was blessed beyond measure.

I encourage you who are in that ugly and seemingly hopeless situation, to see that God wants to use you. He *will* use you if you let Him.

- ✦ You can be used in your hospital bed or in the rest home where you are confined.

- ✦ You can be used in that home where your husband or wife is on a 24-hour-a-day alcoholic binge.

- ✦ You can be used when your spouse is doing everything in his or her power to make life miserable for you.

- ✦ You can be used when your teenage son or daughter tells you, "I hate you!" and proceeds to try to prove it.

- ✦ You can be used when all of your friends are doing drugs and drinking, living morally loose lives, and pressuring you to join them.

✦ You can be used in the midst of your time of discouragement and despair, when nothing you have tried seems to get you out of it.

✦ You can be used *anytime, anywhere, in any situation.*

God is not through using you!

The center of God's will is not only found in the most pleasant situations. In good health. In so-called "ideal" family homes. In times and places where everybody wakes up refreshed and ready to start the new day with a smile and a light heart.

The center of God's will may be in your imprisonment—whatever it is. Your time of captivity can be *well-used* by God, and it can be *well-spent* by you. Your "prison" in no way means that you are not in the center of His will nor does it negate His will being accomplished in your life. I can say from experience that when I have yielded to God and allowed Him to continue to work in my life, the darkest of hours became meaningful, purposeful and ever so much less difficult to get through.

Look what Paul accomplished during his imprisonments. Some of our most beloved Scriptures came out of his time in chains and shackles. What if he had declared himself "useless" for God's purposes?

The problem is this: When we are imprisoned in painful circumstances, we oftentimes stop caring about God's will. We lose interest in being used by Him. It is tempting to just sit down and vegetate (otherwise known as feeling sorry for ourselves!).

We then become part of the problem!

God needs our cooperation to work out His will in our lives, and He needs our willingness to be used by Him. If our response is a resounding *"No,"* we are bound to feel worse and worse. Our prison will grow darker and darker.

If we will say, "Yes God, I'm willing to be used, even here," our darkest hours will become a means to an end. Our prisons will not have gates that keep us in. Instead, we will find that they have gates that let us out! And our release date will come right on time.

Keep on Keeping On!

You will never know what God will bring out of your affliction unless you keep on keeping on. It's easy to give up when the heat is on. But when the furnace gets its hottest, when the prison walls begin to close in, when the pain becomes unbearable, when the enemy is laughing at you—those are the times to keep on keeping on.

Those are the times to look to Jesus and cry out, "Lord, I don't know what You're doing. I don't understand. I don't see anything happening that even resembles something good. But I'm standing firm in the middle of my affliction. I'm believing that You are doing a work that is beyond my understanding."

> I see nothing.
> I hear nothing.
> I feel nothing.
> But I will keep on keeping on.
> Though I may not soar like the eagle;
> Though I may not run like the gazelle;
> I will go on—
> Today, tomorrow and the day after!

My friend, do you know what you have just enabled God to do? You have asked God to not only stand in your prison with you, but you have given Him the go-ahead signal to use your circumstances any way He chooses.

So will He give you a stone for food? No! Will He let your darkest hour be for nothing? No! Will He give the victory to the enemy and allow you to emerge a defeated and winless warrior? No!

God has something better in mind!

God's Drawing Board

Have you ever watched an architect at work, laboriously and tediously working on a blueprint for his client's house? If you have, and if you are as ignorant about architecture as I am, then all of those signs and symbols and angles and arrows are meaningless to you. You might as well be trying to read a foreign language.

But to the skilled architect, every one of those hundreds of marks means something. Every one of them affects the master plan. They each say something to the architect and ultimately to the builder. Only after the architect has done his work and the artist's rendition of that blueprint is painted can the client stand back and look at what the architect had in mind all along.

If I were given the opportunity, I would probably put the blueprint and the artist's painting side by side and, showing my gross ignorance, exclaim, "You mean *that* beautiful house is the product of *that* blueprint?" The irony is that sometimes the more of a "mess" the blueprint appears to be, the more awesome the finished product is!

How I long for you to come to know that God's drawing board has been filled with a blueprint that contains every detail of your life. Each dark corner has its purpose. Each sharp angle is but for the beauty of the finished product. Each room God has drawn has meaning. Even the rooms that look like little prisons. Even those "forever" waiting rooms. Even those areas that look suspiciously like they are intended for testing and trials—endurance chambers, maybe? Yes, even those contribute to the beauty of the finished product.

God's drawing board is filled with designs for beautiful people with beautiful ministries! Consider these:

A blueprint on God's drawing board:
Name: Dave Roever, Naval recruit.
Location: Vietnam.
Situation: Hand grenade explosion.

A blueprint on God's drawing board:
Name: Joni Eareckson, swimmer.
Location: Chesapeake Bay.
Situation: Diving accident—spinal cord injury.

A blueprint on God's drawing board:
Name: Corrie ten Boom, servant of God.
Location: Germany—Ravensbruck Concentration Camp.
Situation: Mass murders. Father and sister died. Horrible evils witnessed day in, day out.

A blueprint on God's drawing board:
Name: Jim Elliot, Nate Saint, Roger Youderian, Ed McCulley, Pete Fleming.
Location: Ecuador—jungle.
Situation: All five murdered by Auca Indians.

Were these blueprints all mistakes? Did God make some gigantic errors? You tell me.

Here is another blueprint on God's drawing board:
Name: (write your name).
Location: (name the place of your darkest hour).
Situation: (name the affliction or the hurt you're going through).

Think carefully. Pray about it. Is your blueprint a mistake? It surely may seem that way to all outward appearances. Your family and friends may be telling you that. But could it be that those "mistakes" are not mistakes at all?

I think, with God's help, you'll discover that your life has a *divine meaning*.

I'm assured by God's Word that your troubles are serving a *divine purpose*.

I believe with all my heart that the story of your every work for Jesus, small or great, will eventually bear the inscription: **Born from affliction.**

– 15 –

Working Through It

✦

All the knowledge in the world about emotional pain will not benefit us if we can't apply it to our own lives. If we cannot take practical steps that will help in our daily walk, even a mountain of information is useless.

This chapter is a "self-help" workbook. Don't worry. It isn't a deep theological study that is way over your head. (I don't know enough to be deeply theological!) But I *have* gone through the school of living and learning, and what I do know is simple, basic and practical.

Someone once told me that he had spoken to a group of scholarly university students about the question: "Is Jesus Christ a living reality? If so, can you prove it?"

I have long remembered his answer to those students. He said, "I have no substance to put before you that proves Jesus Christ is a living reality—*other than myself!* I am the proof, for I have experienced Jesus Christ to be a living reality in my own life. And *that,* no one can take away! You can argue about any facts I might give you, but you cannot take away that which I've experienced.

"And I have experienced Jesus Christ!"

A non-hurting person can read all the books on hurt that have been written. He can listen to hurting people talk about their hurts and how it "hurts to hurt." But until that non-hurting person comes face-to-face with pain in his own life, it will remain but a word with an intellectual definition. It will not become a heartfelt reality.

These practical helps come not only from my thoughts, but also from my heart and from my hurt. I have written them to you, wherever you are right now in the midst of your own difficulties. I've written them from the "nitty-gritty" of having been there, too. In none of these short and simple "self-help" sections am I advising you to do something that I haven't done myself.

I can think of nothing more important than "honesty" as you work on this chapter. We are so used to hiding, disguising, even denying our hurts, it may be a real challenge for you to be totally honest with yourself as you work through these pages. It may be a little scary to expose the hurts that you've borne for so long. It may feel risky to "let it all hang out."

I understand every one of those feelings. But let me encourage you that as new or even as simplistic as these suggestions may seem at first, you will experience a releasing, a cleansing and a healing as you work through the pages that follow.

No one else has to see your efforts. They are between you and the Lord Jesus. If you would rather not write in this book, you may wish to get several sheets of paper and follow the examples.

If this section seems a little too intimidating at first, don't feel that you have to respond to the suggestions. It may be that the Lord would want you to just read through them and think about them. That's okay. All I really want is for you to receive ministry, to know that there is healing for your hurt through the Lord Jesus.

I have received scores of letters from people who write saying that they have never told another soul they are hurting, much less what they are hurting about, and the only reason they wrote to me was because they had read my book, *Satan's Underground*, and they knew I would understand.

The following sections are not written by a psychologist. They are just from the heart of a fellow struggler who is traveling the same road as you and is putting her hand out, saying, "Let's go through this together. We can make it!"

Remember, there are no right or wrong answers. This is not an exercise meant to impress anyone. It is simply a means of expressing, perhaps for the first time, how you *really* feel.

— ✦ —

Coming to Terms with My Hurts

Here are some hurts I would like to work my way through. (Use more paper if necessary.)

1.

2.

3.

4.

5.

I'm sure most of us have more than five hurts in our lives that we have never worked through, but at least this gives us a place to begin.

Which of these sound the most like my responses to hurts?

_____ Continue to evade them, burying them deeper and deeper in an effort to forget them.

_____ Become more and more depressed by dwelling on them.

_____ Try to deal with my hurt by blaming the person who caused my hurt. (The person who hurt you may "deserve" the blame, but the only one who is hurt by blaming them is you.)

_____ Allow myself to remain angry and perhaps even allow hatred to grow in my heart.

_____ Refuse to work on my hurts because "I have a right to feel hurt."

_____ If I had any part in my being hurt, I refuse to acknowledge it.

If you have checked any or all of these statements, it is okay. You have been honest, and God honors your honesty. Look over the statements that you have checked. Think about them. Can you see why you are still hurting?

Most likely your hurt continues to grow bigger and deeper.

When You Talk to God, Be Specific About Your Problem

Generalizations:

"Everything is falling apart."

"Nothing is going right."

"No one understands."

"I can't handle anything anymore."

Generalizations create hopelessness. How can you zero in on a problem when you say that "*everything* is falling apart"? Being specific about the problem narrows it down to a more manageable size. The best way to reduce the hopelessness of the situation is to pinpoint exactly what the problem is.

What are some of the generalizations you make about your problems?

1.

2.

3.

Instead of saying *"Everything* is falling apart," can you narrow these generalizations down and be very specific about each problem?

1. Generalization:

   Specifics: (Name the specific things that are falling apart.)

2. Generalization:

   Specifics:

3. Generalization:

   Specifics:

Now you have some very specific hurts. You have been honest with yourself. It is much easier to talk to God about them because you are talking about single details.

Feelings About Forgiveness

1. Name the hurtful situations. (You may wish to use a separate piece of paper for each hurt.)

2. Check the sentences that describe how you feel about the person who hurt you.

_____ I want to forgive that person, but I can't find it in my heart to forgive him/her.

_____ I don't want to forgive them.

_____ They meant to hurt me, so why should I forgive them?

_____ The least they could do is ask for my forgiveness.

_____ They could at least feel sorry for what they said and did.

_____ Why should I forgive them when they will probably do the same thing again?

_____ Why should I have to still love them? They don't act like they still love me.

_____ Why do I have to change to suit them? Why don't they do some changing?

_____ I'd like to see them get what's coming to them!

Did you make any check marks? Do you know that you need to forgive that person no matter what? Perhaps

you even need to ask God to forgive you for your unforgiveness. Colossians 3:13 exhorts us to "Be gentle
and ready to forgive; never hold grudges." And then it
reminds us that "...the Lord forgave you, so you must
forgive others" (TLB).

"But what if I can't find it in my heart to forgive?" you
ask. "What if I don't know how to forgive them? What if
my hurt is bigger than my ability to forgive?"

The following sentences are a simple prayer that will
start you on the road to forgiveness.

> Help me, Lord Jesus. I still can't forgive
> _____. I still have bad feelings about
> him/her. I have no love in my heart for him/
> her. Will You do what I can't do? Will You
> make me willing to forgive?

As you have prayed this sincerely, you have opened
the door of your heart to the working of the Holy Spirit.
You are on your way!

How Deeply Have You Buried Your Hurt?

I Must:

_____ smile, even though I don't feel like smiling.

_____ keep my hurt to myself.

_____ be strong, even though I feel very weak.

_____ go on about my daily life as though nothing is
wrong.

_____ keep myself in control at all costs!

I Must Not:

_____ shed any tears.

_____ let anyone see my anger, my hurt and my hate, because I know they are sins.

_____ talk about my hurt because:

    _____ People don't want to listen anyway.

    _____ Talking is a sign of being weak.

    _____ What will others think of me?

    _____ I'll be condemned if I talk.

    _____ It won't do any good to talk.

Have you checked any of these statements? Perhaps some of you have made a lot of check marks. Remember, *that's okay*! You're still being honest. There is nothing more important. Just because you have answered in the affirmative to some of these attitudes does not mean your situation is hopeless. It only means that you have listened to the enemy's lies of deception. Of course he would want you to think that it is better to keep all of your hurt inside of you than for you to share it. Because, once you have shared it, it has been exposed to the light of Jesus' healing. Satan surely doesn't want that!

Not to worry! You are now free to *choose* how you will handle your hurts from this point on. True feelings about hurts are never unhealthy as long as you can express them outwardly, allowing the Lord Jesus to bring healing to them.

When the initial wounding happens, feelings, emotions, and thoughts either hit us like an explosion or they creep in silently. We have little, if any, control over our feelings when we are first hurt. They only become unhealthy and unacceptable when we choose to harbor them internally, allowing them to grow and take over our thought life.

> Choosing to deal with my feelings,
> whatever they may be,
> is always healthy!

> Choosing to *not* deal with my feelings,
> whatever they may be,
> is always unhealthy!

Turning a Negative Hurt
Into a Positive Action

The examples below show you the steps you can take in changing negative attitudes and reactions to specific hurts into positive attitudes and reactions. It is a sample work sheet for you to follow in describing reactions toward a specific hurt. After reading these two examples, use other sheets of paper for describing your reactions to the hurts you would like to work on.

Example 1:

Hurt: "It seems that my life has been one disaster after another. Just when I think I am getting over one crisis, something else happens. I am in a vicious circle that keeps me in a continual state of depression. I don't think I even know what it is to be happy anymore!"

Undesired Reaction: "Why keep trying to keep my head above water? It doesn't do any good. Why talk about it? It won't change anything. If this is the way it's always going to be, I might as well resign myself to it."

Desired Reaction: "I know things have been difficult, and they still look bad. I admit that I'm tired of hurting and I'm confused. But I want Jesus to be my all in all. I want to know Him in the midst of every hard place. I want to allow Him to be my strength when I feel so weak."

Steps to Achieving My Goal: "I choose to keep my eyes on Jesus, rather than on my circumstances. I am not avoiding or denying that this unwanted trial exists, but I am rather trusting and believing, asking Jesus to use this time to make me what He wants me to be. I want to be used to comfort someone else when they go through the same trial.

"I will memorize promises from God's Word that mean the most to me, and I will keep going back to them for encouragement and comfort."

Verses like: "I will lift up mine eyes unto the hills from whence cometh my help. My help cometh from the Lord which made heaven and earth"[1]; and "Why are thou cast down, O my soul? and why art thou disquieted within me? hope thou in God: for I shall yet praise him, who is the health of my countenance, and my God."[2]

Example 2:

Hurt: "I have prayed for my husband to get saved for years, but he is still unsaved. If anything, he seems further away from God than ever."

Undesired Reaction: "I keep prodding him (nagging at him) to become a Christian. I go to church all the more, so he will be left alone at home to miss me and be more miserable. I have allowed my unanswered prayer to make me bitter toward the Lord."

Desired Reaction: "I want the beauty and tender love of the Lord Jesus to flow through me to my husband. I want to be loving to him at all times, even in his stubbornness."

Steps to Achieving My Goal: "I shouldn't work on this hurt myself; instead I need to let the Holy Spirit draw my husband to the Lord. I need to pray, 'Lord, love him through me. Do a work in me that will make me more tolerant to his intolerance. And especially Lord, heal my hurt.' "

Now try working on your own examples. As you write down your initial reactions and your desired reactions to your hurts, ask the Lord Jesus to show you *His* solution and the necessary steps toward achieving it. Remember: *There is always a solution in Him!*

Hurt Compounders

"Hurt Compounders" are things you bring or add to your hurt yourself. They are the common responses to being hurt, such as:

guilt	anxiety
self-pity	self-punishment
shame	bitterness
depression	anger
fear	doubt

None of these hurt compounders are part of the hurt itself. They are the common responses that the enemy would just love for you to entertain in the midst of your hurting.

Hurt compounders increase your hurt while they decrease your ability to do anything about it. If you are already struggling and you add any of the hurt compounders to your situation, you are in real trouble!

We cannot avoid all hurt. Troubles, trials, sufferings, pain, losses, afflictions, tragedies—crises of all kinds come into each of our lives. However, we often fall prey to the natural responses of adding unnecessary complications to our crises.

What hurt compounders do you tend to bring or add to your crises?

1.

2.

3.

4.

5.

Now, through prayer, can you confess these emotions to God and ask Him to help you remove them from your heart?

And here's a tip for the future: If you will confess your hurt to Jesus the moment it happens, the enemy won't have a chance to start tossing these hurt compounders into your lap.

I Will Make My Choice

Who is telling you the following things?

Everything is stacked against you.
You'll never make it.
You're guilty.
It's always your fault.
You might as well give up.
Things will never get any better and they'll never change.
What's the use of trying?
This is the way it will always be.
You're going to live and die in your pain.

The master deceiver, the old bully, my enemy is telling me these lies. His name is _____. And he is a liar!

Who is telling you these things?

You are not guilty. You are forgiven!

Come to me, and I will give you peace and rest.
I am the healer of all your hurts.
You are not hopeless, for I am hope.
There is a way out for you.
You are not alone, for I am with you.
I will bring light into your darkness.
You can do all things through me.
I am your life!

The One who loved you enough to die for you. The One who stands with you in your darkest hour. The One who will bear your burdens. His name is _____. And His Word is truth!

I can choose to listen to Satan or to Jesus. No matter how tempting it is to listen to Satan, I choose to listen to and believe Jesus from this moment on!

Jesus says to you, "In all these things we are more than conquerors through him who loved us" (Romans 8:37 NIV).

Name the hurts or situations that you want to be "more than a conqueror" over.

1.

2.

3.

4.

5.

Jesus says that in the midst of the things you just named, you can be conqueror, winner and champion! How? Through Him who loves you! *Not in yourself*, but *in Him*. With Jesus on your side, what can conquer you; what can win over you *without your consent*? Think about it!

In the Midst of My Affliction, What Am I to Do?

1. Don't bear your hurts alone. Give your cares to Jesus and be assured that He cares for you.

   Casting the whole of your care [all your anxieties, all your worries, all your concerns, once and for all] on Him, for He cares for you affectionately and cares about you watchfully (1 Peter 5:7 AMP).

   Ask the Lord Jesus to give you a friend in whom you can confide. "Share each other's troubles and problems, and so obey our Lord's command" (Galatians 6:2 TLB).

2. Keep your mind on Jesus.

   Thou wilt keep him in perfect peace, whose mind is stayed on thee... (Isaiah 26:3 KJV).

3. Run *to* Jesus—not *away* from Him.

   But as for me, I get as close to him as I can! (Psalm 73:28 TLB).

   The one thing I want from God... is the privilege of meditating in his Temple, living in his presence every day of my life.... There I'll be when troubles come (Psalm 27:4,5 TLB).

4. Trust in Jesus' wisdom, even in this trial.

   And now just as you trusted Christ to save you, trust him, too, for each day's problems; live in vital union with him (Colossians 2:6 TLB).

5. Don't become discouraged when you've become weak.

   Even when we are too weak to have any faith left, he remains faithful to us and will help us... (2 Timothy 2:13 TLB).

Now I am glad to boast about how weak I am; I am glad to be a living demonstration of Christ's power . . . for when I am weak, then I am strong—the less I have, the more I depend on him (2 Corinthians 12:9,10 TLB).

6. Rest in Jesus.

Come to me, all you who are weary and burdened, and I will give you rest (Matthew 11:28 NIV).

7. Don't try to stand in your own strength.

It is true that I am an ordinary, weak human being, but I don't use human plans and methods to win my battles. I use God's mighty weapons, not those made by men, to knock down the devil's strongholds (2 Corinthians 10:3,4 TLB).

8. Turn your thoughts away from yourself.

Set your minds on things above, not on earthly things (Colossians 3:2 NIV).

9. Be content even in the darkest hour for Jesus is with you.

. . . I have learned the secret of being content in any and every situation (Philippians 4:13 NIV).

I will not in any way fail you nor give you up nor leave you without support. [I will] not, [I will] not, [I will] not in any degree leave you helpless nor forsake you, nor let [you] down (relax My hold on you)! [Assuredly not!] (Hebrews 13:5 AMP).

10. Don't fear or believe that this period of your life is wasted.

> And we know that in all things God works
> for the good of those who love him . . . (Romans
> 8:28 NIV).

11. Don't call up past sins. Don't dig them out of the
forgiven past and walk in them again.[3]

> As far as the east is from the west, so far
> hath he removed our transgressions from us
> (Psalm 103:12 KJV).

12. Be encouraged that this hurt will not last forever.

> So we do not look at what we can see right
> now, the troubles all around us, but we look
> forward to the joys in heaven which we have
> not yet seen. The troubles will soon be over, but
> the joys to come will last forever (2 Corin-
> thians 4:18 TLB).

We can only have the assurance of the above Scripture
if we know Jesus Christ as the forgiver of our sins and
the Savior of our souls. If you have never made a commitment to Jesus Christ, I invite you to take this step. Jesus
created you so that He could live within you. He wants to
not only be your Savior, but your friend and the healer of
your hurts.

Jesus says, "The one who comes to me I will by no
means cast out" (John 6:37). No matter how hurting you
are, Jesus will not turn you away.

I have found Jesus to be easier to talk to than anyone
else. You will too. For He does not condemn; He forgives.
He does not hurt; He heals. He is never too busy nor too
weary to listen to you. He never tires of your coming to
Him.

If you have just prayed to Him for the first time, and
you would like to sign your name here, this will be a
page you can come back to from now on and say, "This is

the day I asked Jesus to come into my heart, and I became a child of God."

Name: _____

Date: _____

Be Kind to Yourself

Now that you have taken the time to try and work through your pain, it's time for a break. How about trying some of these suggestions for being kind to yourself as you are going through the healing process?

Take a warm bath. At the end of a stress-filled day, relax in a warm bath—after you have put the kids to bed! Put some bubble bath in the water and turn some easy listening music on softly. Sink into the warm water and enjoy!

Watch a favorite video. Laughter is good medicine for the hurting heart. Rent or borrow a "fun" video that's easy to watch and filled with good humor. If you like popcorn (I'm a popcorn fanatic!), pop a bowlful to enjoy while you're watching the video.

Read a book. Whatever your favorite kind of reading is, dust off one of your old favorites or buy that book you've been wanting to read. Take the time out to do it now! Be good to yourself!

Enjoy God's Creation. Sit on your porch or take a walk—not with anyplace special in mind. Just walk and listen and look. Hear the birds chirping. See the brightly-colored flowers. Watch some boys playing catch. Hear their laughter. Notice the simple joys that Jesus has created.

Make a cup of coffee. Buy some special coffee beans. Grind them yourself and smell the fragrant aroma as it's brewing. Then relax in your favorite chair. Put your feet up and enjoy your freshly-poured cup of coffee.

Ride a bike. No, I don't mean a motorcycle, unless that's your preference! How long has it been since you've been on a bicycle? I'm not kidding! Try it. You will be amazed at how it makes you feel—young and carefree with the wind blowing through your hair. Besides, it's good exercise!

Be sure to eat right! At this point I have to say, "Do as I say, not as I do!" But I have found that a bowl sitting on my counter filled with fruits in colors of orange and yellow and red and green is awfully tempting! They are not only enjoyable to eat, but they are nutritious.

Buy some art supplies. "Are you kidding? I can't draw," you protest. Neither can I, believe me. But you would be surprised how therapeutic it is to use crayons, or water-colors or a charcoal pencil. Draw anything. It doesn't have to look like something, and you don't have to show it to anyone. Create on your canvas the feelings of your heart. It can be a surprising step of healing for you.

Listen to worship music. You might even hum along with it. For me, I know of nothing more relaxing and comforting than getting somewhere all by myself and quietly listening to tapes of worship music. You can purchase them at any Christian bookstore. I have a portable cassette player with headphones. I find a favorite place to be, perhaps in a park or just lying on the floor, and I ask Jesus to minister to me through His music. And He does!

Go for a drive. Out in the country, preferably. Away from crowded freeways, stoplights, exhaust fumes and honking horns. Drive slowly. Don't forget to watch the road, but take in the beauty of the hills, the trees, the little animals—maybe rabbits or owls or birds sitting on fences. It's good to get away from the city once in a while!

And when you can't take another step,

Go to bed! A hurting person tends to keep busy all day and way into the night hours. But we can't do it all in one day, and there is always tomorrow. I have a bad habit of pushing myself beyond my limit. Trouble is, I don't get anything done even if I do stay up half the night! Finally a caring friend suggested, firmly but kindly, "Go to bed, Lauren!" It's true. We need our rest. God will tend to our bodies and our hearts as we sleep in His care.

Be kind to yourself!

Have fun!

Enjoy simple things!

And don't forget to laugh!

My Resolution

"I will not dwell on my hurt. I choose to take my eyes off my hurt. I choose to be good to myself. I choose to look to God who can lift me above my hurt."

An Ending Prayer

"Dear Father, I'm hurting so badly. But in the midst of my pain and hurt, I choose to give it all to You. As I express each of my hurts to You, I ask You to take them and to begin a work of healing in my heart.

"I know that hurt will come into my life again. But help me bring it to You the moment it happens so You can pour Your healing balm of ointment over it. Amen."

The Lord lifts the fallen
and those bent beneath their loads
(Psalm 145:14 TLB).

– Epilogue –

New Healings

✦

Since the writing of my autobiography, *Satan's Underground*, the Lord Jesus has brought some exciting experiences into my recovery. There are new healings going on in my life, day after day, month after month. And I want you to know about them—things like riding a bicycle!

"Come on now," you're probably saying. "What's so new about riding a bicycle?"

Well, for one thing, it's a miracle!

Physically, I was confined to a wheelchair for many months. Then I graduated to crutches. Then to a cane. Riding a bicycle was once an absolute impossibility. Today it has been made physically possible through the healing touch of Jesus.

And emotionally? I'm even more excited about that! When I climbed on that bicycle seat and started rather shakily down the driveway, I felt like a little girl—carefree, happy, and normal—for the first time in my life!

I had never before felt like a little girl, even when I was a child. That child was never carefree, happy or normal. Never, that is, until a few months ago. As the wind blew on my face and through my hair, I thought, *So this is what it's like to really be a little girl!* At the end of each day as I've been writing the manuscript for *I Know You're Hurting*, I have gotten on my bicycle and taken a short ride. And each day, another part of that little girl has been touched by the Master's hand.

If you have read *Satan's Underground*, you know what wonderful things Jesus has wrought!

So . . . can you guess what I want to do next? I want to go to a park and ride on a swing! Do you know why? I have never been on a swing. I have always avoided playgrounds, because of the pain they brought to my heart.

But I rode my bicycle to a park near my house a few days ago, and watched the children for awhile. My eyes were drawn to one little girl with long, blonde hair, giggling and squealing with delight as she swung higher and higher into the air. Oh my, how carefree! How happy! "I want to do that, too," I heard myself whisper. Then out of the corner of my eye I noticed two little boys on a teeter-totter. They were having so much fun. "That too!" I said out loud.

A miracle is taking place, and I'm really getting well! You see, until a few months ago, I avoided children at all costs. I went out of my way to avoid baby dedications at church. One dedication sort of sneaked up on me by surprise. I tried to sit through it, but I didn't quite make it. I held my hurt in for so long, and then I just jumped up and ran outside. I leaned against the wall of the church in the parking lot and wept. My memories just weren't healed.

I avoided baby showers. I avoided driving by playgrounds. I never volunteered to work in the church nursery. Just seeing a mother walking hand in hand with her little girl brought stabs of pain to my heart.

And now I am riding a bicycle like a child! I want to swing on a swing and ride (or whatever it is you do) on a teeter-totter!

That's not all. Even a very personable, gentlemanly cat named Maxwell has filled a long-empty place in my life. Of course I never had a pet when I was a child, and you can't imagine what joy my feline friend has brought to me.

In short, if you could imagine what wonders Jesus is working all around me, you would stand up and cheer!

These are new healings the Lord is continuing to administer to my deeply-buried hurts. He's especially working on inner wounds I incurred as a child through rejection, neglect, and physical and sexual abuse. I encourage you who have been too afraid to deal with these kinds of wounds to ask the Lord if He will take you through this kind of healing, too. It's painless and it's fun! Only one catch—I think it will only be effective if the Lord is directing it in *His* perfect time.

Some of this may sound childish and maybe even embarrassing to you. But for me, it is possibly the most adult thing I have ever done. For it has accomplished what I could not—the healing of the very scared and deeply hurting little girl who has been crying for help year after year after year. Praise be to Jesus, her cry is being answered by her loving and gentle Heavenly Father.

My Brand-New Birth Family

You read in the first chapter about the deep hurt I went through a couple of years ago when I learned who my birth parents were, and why my birth mother wanted to give me away. The devastation of hurt and bitterness and anger didn't subside. It grew more intense as time went by. It was one hurt for which I thought I would never find healing.

I made the comment that this one hurt was "beyond healing"—that I was broken by it "beyond repair." I described myself as "unrescuable," and I wrote that "I could do nothing more than place my brokenness in His Hands."

Well, let me tell you something. As I watched God do

the impossible of beginning to heal the little girl in me, I decided that maybe, *just maybe*, God could heal the oldest hurt of all, the one that began at birth. He has begun to do just that! But there has been both a "downside" and an "upside" to this healing.

My birth mother and father did get married, but wanted no children. So I have no brothers or sisters. My father committed suicide when I was twelve years of age, and my mother died several years ago. I had hoped to get the chance to visit my birth parents' graves before I finished writing this book so I could include another paragraph on the healing of that hurt. I was unable to do so, but I will be going as soon as this book is finished.

The upside is that I have had the extreme privilege and joy of meeting a few of my birth relatives. There are several aunts, uncles and a host of cousins. It hurt them deeply to read *Satan's Underground*, to discover what happened to me after I was given away. But they are a hardy family and have dealt with the tragic story astonishingly well.

My aunts and cousins have been wonderful! They have given me permission to use their names in this book, but I have decided not to. I don't want their lives interrupted or harassed in any way. Still, it meant a lot to me that they were willing to see their names connected with mine.

One of my cousins looks very much like me. Several of us have the same talents. I guess talents are inherited after all! And I finally know what it is to look into the face of another human being who is actually related to me.

All this happened because, with God's help, I was able to confront possible rejection and a consuming fear and dread of the unknown.

I have asked my sister, Johanna, who saw me through to freedom and about whom I write in the last chapters of *Satan's Underground*, to let you see from her perspective how she has seen God's faithfulness in healing a very hurting person—*me*. We can be encouraged by her words.

— ◆ —

In March of 1986, I met a broken woman—a woman who seemed to be shattered beyond all hope of restoration or repair. For hour after hour, week after week, Lauren huddled in my arms whispering and sobbing out the most heart-wrenching story I had ever heard. It hardly seemed possible that anyone could have survived the horrors and anguish she described. Her emotional pain was compounded by unrelenting physical pain from an incurable blood disorder. Even her doctor, whom I met, was amazed she was still alive.

And yet as month after month passed, the woman whom I had come to love as a sister began to get better! Beyond all expectations, she graduated from her wheelchair to crutches to a cane. Now she walks with none at all!

Her illness has not, as yet, been cured, but she has shown miraculous improvement. Lauren would be the first to tell you that despite the "thorn in her flesh," God's grace has been and will continue to be her sufficiency. And whether or not God chooses to heal her, she is complete in Him!

But the greatest healing I have seen in my sister is not physical, but mental and spiritual. When we first met, Lauren was in the gripping bondage of fear. Her will, broken and conditioned through the long years of abuse, steadily grew stronger as she came to understand she had the right to say "No!" No to the abuse, the brainwashing techniques, the guilt, the hatred, and especially to remaining a victim. No to every technique her abusers had used to control her. Even no to Satan himself!

I have watched her spirit heal as she made deliberate choices which said "Yes!" to God's will for her life. She chose to forgive all those who so deliberately, so viciously, so methodically sought the destruction of her mind, her spirit and her body; and to let go of the role of victim, in which she had been captive for so many years. *In Jesus* she has become *more than conqueror.*

Those choices were not made without tears, and her healing has not happened overnight. Some of those choices must still be worked through at new levels, renewed and even made again from time to time. The wounds and anger of a lifetime are not easily relinquished. But I am convinced that it was Lauren's determination to grow close to the Lord Jesus Christ and in His Name bring encouragement to others, that has played a crucial part in the process of her healing. Since I have known my sister, the cry of her heart has been for those who are hurting—for those who don't yet know that there is hope, life, freedom, and yes, even joy and laughter in Christ Jesus.

The frightened, hopeless woman I knew three-and-a-half years ago is now a determined and courageous warrior. She is living proof that God, indeed, works all things together for good for those who love Him and are called according to His purpose.

—Johanna Michaelsen

— ✦ —

I want you to know that God not only can, but He *will* do the same thing for you. Yes, I am special to Him. *But so are you!*

The two areas of my life I have feared the most have begun to be healed since I have started this book. I wrote in the preface of this book that I feared having to live through many of the things I would be writing about. It has been difficult, yes. But what a beautiful time of healing I have had—opening up areas of hurt through my writing that I have never been willing to give to Jesus before.

He is truly perfecting that which concerns me!

I encourage you once again, you who are too hurt and too fearful to deal with the deepest of your hurts, to trust them to Jesus. *I know because I know.* I've experienced it. I've lived it. I've proven it:

> *Jesus is faithful to heal*
> *the hurts of the worst kind.*
> *No hurt is beyond his healing!*

Heal me, O Lord, and I shall be healed
(Jeremiah 17:14 KJV).

— ✦ —

Notes

Chapter 2
1. June Hunt, "Surrendered," 1987.

Chapter 5
1. Phillipians 4:7 (KJV).

Chapter 6
1. The Boys Town Center in Boys Town, Nebraska, in cooperation with the National PTA, Chicago, IL, states the statistical findings that of runaways between 17 years-of-age and under, only 5 percent of them attempt to run away under the age of 12.
2. Marie Chapian, *His Thoughts Toward Me* (Bethany House Publishers, 1987), p. 135.
3. H.G.B., "Our Daily Bread" (Radio Bible Class), n.d.

Chapter 8
1. Chuck Swindoll, *For Those Who Hurt* (Multnomah Press, 1977).
2. Swindoll, *For Those Who Hurt.*

Chapter 9
1. Joyce Landorf Heatherley, *Your Dear Face* (Austin, TX: Balcony Publishing, 1984).

Chapter 10
1. M.R. DeHaan II, "Job: The Great Debate" (Radio Bible Class, 1982), p. 10.

Chapter 11
1. Edith Schaeffer, *Affliction* (Fleming H. Revell Co., 1978), p. 28.
2. Chapian, *His Thoughts Toward Me*, p. 29.

Chapter 12
1. Schaeffer, *Affliction*, p. 62.
2. Ibid.

Chapter 13
1. Schaeffer, *Affliction*, p. 169.
2. Matthew Henry, *The Matthew Henry Commentary* (Zondervan Publishing House, 1961), p. 1836.
3. Schaeffer, *Affliction*, p. 152.

Chapter 14
1. *The Hiding Place* is a film about Corrie ten Boom's life.
2. Corrie ten Boom, *Each New Day* (Spire Books, 1977), p. 110.
3. Yogi Berra, *Yogi* (McGraw Hill, 1989).
4. Orphan diseases are ones which are so rare that very little is known about them.
5. Orphan drugs are ones which are in such little demand that drug companies don't want to manufacture them because there is no profit in it.

Chapter 15
1. Psalm 121:1,2 (KJV).
2. Psalm 42:11 (KJV).
3. Chapian, *His Thoughts*, p. 131.

RECOMMENDED READING

Arthur, Kay, *Lord, Heal My Hurts* (Portland: Multnomah Press, 1988).

Buhler, Rich, *Pain and Pretending* (Nashville: Thomas Nelson Publishers, 1988).

Chapian, Marie, *His Gifts to Me* (Minneapolis: Bethany House Publishers, 1988).

Chapian, Marie, *His Thoughts Toward Me* (Minneapolis: Bethany House Publishers, 1987).

Hansel, Tim, *You Gotta Keep Dancin'* (Elgin: David C. Cook, 1985).

Heatherley, Joyce Landorf, *Silent September* (Austin: Balcony Publishing, 1984).

Omartian, Stormie, *Stormie* (Eugene, OR: Harvest House Publishers, 1986).

Rankin, Peg, *Yet Will I Trust Him* (Ventura: Regal Books, 1980).

Roever, Dave, *Welcome Home, Davey* (Waco: Word Books, 1986).

Schaeffer, Edith, *Affliction* (Old Tappan: Fleming H. Revell Co., 1978).

Swindoll, Charles, *Encourage Me* (Portland, OR: Multnomah Press, 1982).

Swindoll, Charles, *For Those Who Hurt* (Portland, OR: Multnomah Press, 1977).

Tada, Joni Eareckson, *Glorious Intruder* (Portland, OR: Multnomah Press, 1989).

✦ The Living Bible, Paraphrased (Wheaton, IL: Tyndale Publishers, 1971).

✦ There are many good versions of the Bible, but when I am hurting, I always pick up The Living Bible. For you who are unfamiliar with the Bible, I urge you to begin reading in the Book of Psalms, found in the Old Testament portion of the Bible.

Dear Reader:

We would appreciate hearing from you regarding this Harvest House nonfiction book. It will enable us to continue to give you the best in Christian publishing.

1. What most influenced you to purchase *I Know You're Hurting*?
   - ☐ Author
   - ☐ Subject matter
   - ☐ Backcover copy
   - ☐ Recommendations
   - ☐ Cover/Title
   - ☐ _____

2. Where did you purchase this book?
   - ☐ Christian bookstore
   - ☐ General bookstore
   - ☐ Department store
   - ☐ Grocery store
   - ☐ Other

3. Your overall rating of this book:
   ☐ Excellent ☐ Very good ☐ Good ☐ Fair ☐ Poor

4. How likely would you be to purchase other books by this author?
   - ☐ Very likely
   - ☐ Somewhat likely
   - ☐ Not very likely
   - ☐ Not at all

5. What types of books most interest you?
   (check all that apply)
   - ☐ Women's Books
   - ☐ Marriage Books
   - ☐ Current Issues
   - ☐ Self Help/Psychology
   - ☐ Bible Studies
   - ☐ Fiction
   - ☐ Biographies
   - ☐ Children's Books
   - ☐ Youth Books
   - ☐ Other _____

6. Please check the box next to your age group.
   - ☐ Under 18
   - ☐ 18-24
   - ☐ 25-34
   - ☐ 35-44
   - ☐ 45-54
   - ☐ 55 and over

Mail to: Editorial Director
Harvest House Publishers
1075 Arrowsmith
Eugene, OR 97402

Name _____

Address _____

City _____ State _____ Zip _____

**Thank you for helping us to help you
in future publications!**